Janu

Day by Day
with
God

Rooting women's lives in the Bible

BRF

The Bible Reading Fellowship
15 The Chambers, Vineyard
Abingdon OX14 3FE
brf.org.uk

The Bible Reading Fellowship (BRF) is a Registered Charity (233280)

ISBN 978 0 85746 999 1
All rights reserved

This edition © 2020 The Bible Reading Fellowship
Cover image © iStock.com/torwai

Distributed in Australia by:
MediaCom Education Inc, PO Box 610, Unley, SA 5061
Tel: 1 800 811 311 | admin@mediacom.org.au

Distributed in New Zealand by:
Scripture Union Wholesale, PO Box 760, Wellington
Tel: 04 385 0421 | suwholesale@clear.net.nz

Acknowledgements
Scripture quotations marked with the following abbreviations are taken from the version shown. Where no abbreviation is given, the quotation is taken from the same version as the headline reference. ESV: The Holy Bible, English Standard Version, published by HarperCollins Publishers, © 2001 Crossway Bibles, a division of Good News Publishers. Used by permission. All rights reserved. NIV: The Holy Bible, New International Version (Anglicised edition) copyright © 1979, 1984, 2011 by Biblica. Used by permission of Hodder & Stoughton Publishers, a Hachette UK company. All rights reserved. 'NIV' is a registered trademark of Biblica. UK trademark number 1448790. NCV: New Century Version (NCV) The Holy Bible, New Century Version®. Copyright © 2005 by Thomas Nelson, Inc. GW: GOD'S WORD Translation (GW) Copyright © 1995 by God's Word to the Nations. Used by permission of God's Word Mission Society. NLT: The Holy Bible, New Living Translation, copyright © 1996, 2004, 2007, 2013. Used by permission of Tyndale House Publishers, Inc., Carol Stream, Illinois 60188. All rights reserved.

Every effort has been made to trace and contact copyright owners for material used in this resource. We apologise for any inadvertent omissions or errors, and would ask those concerned to contact us so that full acknowledgement can be made in the future.

A catalogue record for this book is available from the British Library

Printed and bound by Gutenberg Press, Tarxien, Malta

Day by Day
with
God

Edited by **Jill Rattle**   **January–April 2021**

Writers in this issue

Chine McDonald is head of media and PR at Christian Aid. She read theology and religious studies at Cambridge before training as a newspaper journalist. She is a regular contributor to BBC religion and ethics programmes. Chine is the author of *Am I Beautiful?* – a book exploring body image among Christian women.

Rachel Turner is the Parenting for Faith Pioneer at BRF. Over the past 15 years she has worked across a variety of denominations as a children's, youth and family life pastor. She is the author of six books. **parentingforfaith.org**

Sheila Jacobs is a writer, an editor and an award-winning author. She is also a day chaplain at a retreat house and a retreat leader. She loves encouraging new writers and facilitating a space for people to meet with Jesus.

Rosemary Green has written for BRF since 1992. She enjoyed 61 years of shared ministry with her husband Michael before his death in 2019. She has four adult offspring, 14 grandchildren and two great-grandchildren. Her main ministry is among seniors in her own church in Abingdon.

Jennifer Rees Larcombe runs Beauty from Ashes, an organisation that supports people adjusting to bereavement and trauma. She lives in the Kentish countryside with her little dog Noah and loves gardening and entertaining her 15 grandchildren.

Fiona Barnard is a TEFL/ESOL teacher and staff member of Friends International. She works with international students, encouraging local Christians to reach out in friendship and evangelism to make disciples. She is an honorary chaplain at the University of St Andrews, Scotland.

Hannah Fytche read theology at Cambridge and worked recently at St Andrew's Church in Chesterton. She's passionate about seeing God's love transform lives and communities, and embraces this passion through writing, speaking and spending time with friends and family.

Nell Goddard is church partnerships manager at International Justice Mission (IJM) UK, a freelance writer and an editor. She is the author of *Musings of a Clergy Child: Growing into a faith of my own* (BRF, 2017).

Amy Boucher Pye is a writer, speaker and retreat leader who runs the *Woman Alive* book club. She's the author of the award-winning *Finding Myself in Britain* (Authentic, 2015) and *The Living Cross* (BRF, 2016). **amyboucherpye.com**

Jill Rattle writes...

Are you a runner? The imagery of a race in Hebrews 12 reminds us that we're all 'runners' who must press on, our eyes focused firmly on the goal: Jesus himself. It pictures us as individual runners who shouldn't be distracted by others around us. But there is another sort of race we Christians take part in – a team race where one runner, after her lap, passes the baton on to the next team member. One lap builds on the previous one until the race is finished.

After this issue of *Day by Day with God*, I'm passing on the editorial baton to Jackie Harris, the former editor of *Woman Alive* magazine. Jackie is going to run a strong lap until it's her turn to pass the baton on again. I feel so privileged to have been part of the team.

As Christians we are each given, by God himself, a lifetime of ministries, some short, some long. We have the amazing privilege of working with him, in both big and small ways, to establish his kingdom here on earth. Ephesians 2:10 (ESV) says: 'For we are his workmanship, created in Christ Jesus for good works, which God prepared beforehand, that we should walk in them.'

How good to know that Jesus has *prepared beforehand* those things he wants us to do with him. And how important it is to consider prayerfully whether something we are currently doing *has* been prepared for us by Jesus or whether we should stop because it's actually someone else's job! Perhaps there would be less Christian burnout if we got better at discerning that.

The great thing about laying down one baton is that God always has a new one for us to pick up. God is the God of the new, of renewal, of new experiences to show us and share with us. In our reading of the Bible, the Holy Spirit constantly refreshes our understanding of God and leads us into new encounters with him.

For me, reading Rachel Turner's notes on the theology of God in the darkness was one such encounter. I hope that as you read the contributions in this issue day by day, you too will have some beautiful refreshing times with God. And as you approach Easter, may you be gripped again by the wonder of his cross and his resurrection, bringing you new life!

A very human story: Psalms Books 3–4

Chine McDonald writes:

I love books. Every room in our house includes bookshelves stacked with books whose pages contain stories about humanity's place in the world, about politics, art and faith, and about love, loss, hope and despair. For me, the stories that resonate most are those in which the heroes are not one-dimensional. It is important to me that they convey a depth of personality, experiences and emotions – because humans are complicated. So is life.

I love the psalms because they convey the complexity of human beings, full of contradictions. I love the psalms because they do not pretend that loving and following God means you never question or get angry at him for not intervening when things are going badly. Each psalm offers different perspectives and situations that we can individually relate to. This is why the psalms are among the most quoted Bible passages for Christians, and it's significant that the psalms are some of the most quoted scripture passages in the New Testament.

I love the psalms because they convey so many aspects of human experience – from despair and hopelessness to wonder and praise. The writers describe wrestling with God and struggling with life, and they show us how, despite all difficulties, we can be in relationship with God and dwell in his presence.

The psalms are split up into five books, each ending with a doxology – a form of praise to God. Books 3 and 4, which we will explore over the next few days, are rich in their demonstration of some of the most profound experiences humans can have. Book 3 is full of lamentation and complaint at God's judgement. It is heartening to see the authenticity of the writers of the psalms, who express the full range of emotions, including anger, indignation and lament, but also joy. Book 4 explores the place of a fragile and broken humanity within the sovereignty of God.

May the following few notes help you exhale – breathing out in the knowledge that you are not alone – and inhale the life of the Spirit to spur you on to a deeper relationship with God.

New beginnings: ever-faithful God

Whom have I in heaven but you? And earth has nothing I desire besides you. My flesh and my heart may fail, but God is the strength of my heart and my portion forever. (NIV)

I read an article recently that perfectly described the burden that many women feel when it comes to juggling all the balls that society throws us – employee, employer, church leader, mother, wife, friend, carer. It described the 'mental load' that many women feel – the relentless thoughts that swirl around in the back of our minds.

For me, I juggle a more-than-full-time job with other assignments, but I am also constantly thinking about what to serve for dinner, how my son is doing at nursery, the people I need to check in on, the birthday presents I need to buy and how to be a great wife. Sometimes it all gets a bit too much.

Often the weekend becomes not a time for relaxing and recuperating, but the time when we try to work through the to-do lists while at the same time adding to them. The physical toll is never-ending and we can become exhausted.

If you feel anything like me, today – the start of a brand-new year – is the perfect time to meditate on today's passage. It is a recognition that, though our hearts and bodies may fail and become weary from all the things we have to do, we have the privilege of being able to rely on the king of heaven. Who have we but him? Perhaps this year we should take up the challenge to draw much nearer to God, recognising that it is good for us to do so. For he is our refuge. It is in him we can find the strength that we need, not just to survive, but to thrive, living life in all its fullness.

Consider carving out time over the next few months for a solo retreat, taking time out to rest, recuperate and meditate on the goodness of God.

CHINE MCDONALD

I will remember

I thought about the former days, the years of long ago; I remembered my songs in the night. (NIV)

The end of a year is always a time when we reflect on the twelve months that have passed: we look back at the successes, the failures, the friends and loved ones departed and the new lives begun. It can be a time when we celebrate all the good that has happened; but it can also be a time for disappointment at our failures – those things that we had resolved to do at the start of the year and didn't. We're disappointed that the year has not turned out as we had hoped.

As you reflect on the start of last year, perhaps there were things you prayed God would do for you or your loved ones – healing from physical or mental illnesses, breakthroughs in work situations, restored relationships with others. When we don't see answers, we're tempted to question God or even be angry at him. Reading today's passage at the start of a new year gives us an opportunity to remind ourselves not of what God hasn't done for us, but of what he has.

In these verses, the psalmist remembers the past, the troubled situations they have experienced, and they question God's provision. In times of difficulty, it can be easy to forget what God has done, to wonder whether he will ever show favour again and whether his compassion will return.

We can choose, however, at the start of this new year to remember God's promises, as the psalmist eventually does after this period of doubt. God is faithful – yesterday, today and forever. When things seem bleak and difficult, we should intentionally remember those times when 'the Most High stretched out his right hand'. Remembering his miracles of long ago will move us towards praise and make us more confident in the future.

Take time to reflect on those moments when you felt God's presence in the middle of difficult situations; write them down and give thanks for his provision.

CHINE MCDONALD

In his presence

How lovely is your dwelling-place, Lord Almighty! My soul yearns, even faints, for the courts of the Lord; my heart and my flesh cry out for the living God. (NIV)

A few months ago, my husband and I moved from our new-build flat to the Edwardian house we had always dreamed of living in. There have definitely been times since when I've regretted our decision. I remember the first evening in our new home. After the stresses of packing and moving, and after the removals company had left, we sat alone – my husband, son and I – in a cold, draughty and neglected shell of a house.

Over the months, however, I have found myself really enjoying transforming it into a home – a space that we do not just occupy, but in which we dwell. I've loved poring over the interior-design magazines and Pinterest boards and watching home-improvement shows to see how others have achieved their renovations. There are particular moments in which I have felt that our house is *home* – for example, when we have welcomed our friends and family in to eat or stay with us. It is in the exchanges across the dining table as we tuck into delicious meals, the knowing nods of understanding over hot cups of tea, the chaotic running around after small children, that we feel most in relationship with each other and 'at home'.

Today's passage reminds us of how lovely it is when we dwell in God's courts. While I'm on a trip away, I can yearn for home and there is so much joy when I return. In the same way, when we have spent time outside the 'courts of the Lord', our souls can yearn and faint for that holy place. What a wonderful homecoming it is when we re-enter his presence.

Father, thank you that you invite us – broken as we are – into your courts. What a privilege it is to enter your presence. Thank you for your grace upon us.
CHINE MCDONALD

A divine story (1): lament

Relent, Lord! How long will it be? Have compassion on your servants. Satisfy us in the morning with your unfailing love, that we may sing for joy and be glad all our days. (NIV)

So often we read the psalms in isolation. I have found myself returning to certain verses depending on how I am feeling or which situation in my life I am working through. But reading psalms in isolation rather than taking a more holistic overview can make us miss some profound truths or the beauty that comes with recognising a journey told through these passages.

Today is the first of three reflections on a three-part story told in Psalms 90—92. Today's reflection tells the story of lament; tomorrow's, of divine promise; and the following day's, of thanksgiving.

As I read today's verses from Psalm 90, I'm reminded of those really difficult periods in my life – when I've despaired at doors that have been shut, feared of being forever lonely or experienced the tragedies of the untimely death of loved ones. During such times, it is natural to ask God to give us a break, to show compassion and to have mercy on us. We yearn for God to turn our mourning into dancing, and sometimes it seems like God is not hearing us. This prayer of Moses feels like familiar ground when things are difficult. It is a bold plea to a divine creator, a desperate cry for him to turn things around on our behalf.

Sometimes in the middle of the darkness, it is hard to believe that things will ever be different – but in relationship with God we can take comfort in the fact that he is big enough to handle our desperate cries and to hold our hand through it all. He also sends us glimmers of hope through his promises, which we begin to see at the end of today's passage.

Father God, thank you that you do not abandon us in times of trouble, but hold our hands through the difficult times.

CHINE MCDONALD

A divine story (2): promise

Whoever dwells in the shelter of the Most High will rest in the shadow of the Almighty. I will say of the Lord, 'He is my refuge and my fortress, my God, in whom I trust.' (NIV)

The Bible is full of the promises of God to us. These promises can give us much-needed hope in times of trouble. Reflecting on the situations in which I have felt most in need of God's assurance, I recall being full of doubt as to whether God would actually fulfil his promises.

Some years ago, when I was single and very much did not want to be, some dear friends prayed for me and they gave me a word they believed was from God, that I would marry and have children. At that moment, from where I was standing, this promise seemed so unbelievably ridiculous. But just three years later, I was married, and not very long after that I had my first child. That to me is the most obvious example in my life of a promise from God being fulfilled.

But I'm also painfully aware of hopes not fulfilled either in my own life or in friends' lives, despite much prayer and relentlessly clinging to God's promises. Being in relationship with God plainly does not mean that all our wishes will come true, but it does provide an ultimate hope in the midst of the pain and uncertainty that life throws at us.

Today's passage powerfully conveys God's profound promises to his people and speaks of the refuge and protection that is found only in him, 'my fortress… in whom I trust'. By standing firm on his promises and resting 'in the shadow of the Almighty', we take our eyes off the present realities and fix them on the everlasting God, who never fails.

Spend some time today looking up some of God's promises. You could start with Exodus 14:14, Isaiah 41:10 and Philippians 4:19.

CHINE MCDONALD

A divine story (3): thanksgiving

For you make me glad by your deeds, Lord; I sing for joy at what your hands have done. How great are your works, Lord, how profound your thoughts! (NIV)

And so it was that I found myself dancing up the aisle at a Methodist church in rural Nigeria, my husband, toddler and I surrounded by around 50 family members, a goat, some yams and wads of cash. Dressed in white, we danced up the aisle to place our offerings at the altar of the church to give thanks to God for the birth of our son. It had been some years since I had been in Nigeria – where my family is from – and we were gathered there from all over the world for a few days to bury my grandmother. Nigerians know how to do ritual with wonderful exuberance. My grandmother's homegoing was a wonderful affair, with hundreds gathered from all over the country to pay their respects.

The day after her funeral, we had agreed to take part in a thanksgiving service to show our gratitude to God for the new life of our son – the event was to symbolise how God can turn our mourning into dancing. That thanksgiving service was a joyous affair; it made me realise the importance of giving thanks for all the good things we receive from God's hand. So often, our prayers can be shopping lists, symbolising our dissatisfactions and disappointments. But God has done so much for us. What can we do but praise him?

I would love to have heard what the song of thanksgiving described in Psalm 92 sounded like. I'm sure it would have been a joyful sound. What a hopeful end to this divine story – from lament, to the promises of God, to thanksgiving for all he has done.

May we be people who always choose to praise him. May he be forever exalted!
CHINE MCDONALD

Here we are to worship

Come, let us sing for joy to the Lord; let us shout aloud to the Rock of our salvation. Let us come before him with thanksgiving and extol him with music and song. (NIV)

I have always loved worship music. In fact, as a little girl, I would sit alone in my room and sing through church song and hymn books. I loved the variety of worship music styles – from pop-rock to gospel to classical, reflecting the wonderful fact that people have always found new ways of worshipping God in their own times, cultures and contexts.

Studies have shown the benefits of communal singing and what it does for our health and well-being – whether or not the music is Christian in nature. But wonderful things happen when God's people gather together in sung worship, something that even the best karaoke night or community choir group cannot replicate. Some of the moments when I have most tangibly felt the presence of God have been within those times of communal worship, when voices are lifted towards heaven in praise.

The psalms are full of passages that are familiar to us today not least because they are quoted in some of the world's best-known worship songs. Today's reading is another familiar one and, in reading it again, I am struck by the sense of a rallying call. The worship of God in this passage is intentional: it calls on God's people to *choose* worship – to sing for joy, to shout aloud, to come before God with music and song. It is a reminder that whatever else might be going on in our lives, 'let us' always make time to worship God because of who he is.

For he alone is worthy of all our praise, of all our attention; he alone is the one upon whom we should cast and focus our gaze.

Father God, you are worthy to be praised. Thank you for who you are. Help us to be a people of worship.

CHINE MCDONALD

Love abounds

The Lord is compassionate and gracious, slow to anger, abounding in love. (NIV)

There are moments when I look into my son's eyes, when he curls his little fingers around mine or when he runs towards me when he sees me, that I am overwhelmed with love. It's a heart-thumping love that at times takes my breath away. I cannot imagine anything more perfect. But as much as I love him, there are also times when I'm shocked at how frustrated I can get with him: when he is up for hours in the night, when he throws his food off the high chair or when he lets out an ear-piercing scream. It's amazing how quickly I can move from love to frustration to anger; how seamless the transition between adoration and exasperation! It's in these moments that I do not feel I am showing the compassion to my child that a parent should.

The Bible is full of the metaphor of God as Father, including the story Jesus told of the prodigal son, which could perhaps be better titled 'The parable of the forgiving father'. I'm so thankful that Jesus shows us that God is slow to anger and always abounding in love. It is such a relief when we recognise the utter joy God has in us, his children. Though we may be frustrating, though we may return again and again to our sinful nature, though we may not love our brothers and sisters as we should, God's love and forgiveness abounds.

When I am quick to be angry and frustrated at even those I love most in the world, I pray that I would be reminded of God's unfailing grace and love towards me.

Gracious and compassionate God, forgive us for the times when we have not shown love to others. May we live in the light of your love for us.

CHINE MCDONALD

A beautiful creation

**How many are your works, Lord! In wisdom you made them all;
the earth is full of your creatures. There is the sea, vast and spacious,
teeming with creatures beyond number – living things both large
and small. (NIV)**

Over the holidays, I have been immersed in the wondrous life of toddler-hood. It has been amazing to watch my two-year-old's extraordinary development, to listen to the new words he has been adding to his vocabulary and to nurture his growing independence.

One of the most magical things about being a parent to a young child is being immersed in and sharing their favourite stories. Over the past few weeks I have heard the story of *The Snail and the Whale* over and over again. This beautiful book by Julia Donaldson and its film adaptation tell the tale of the unlikely friendship between a tiny sea snail and a majestic humpback whale. As the two explore the world together, their eyes are opened to the beauty of nature – the wondrous, 'vast and spacious' sea spoken of in today's passage.

Stopping and taking time to pause and reflect on nature in all its diversity is something that can inspire us and nurture our walk with God; it can also help us to celebrate the beauty of this diversity – not just in the natural world, but also in the communities in which we live.

We grown-ups need to experience the childlike wonder of seeing God's glory reflected in creation. It is this wonder that can remind us afresh of how great our God is and how he is greatly to be praised. Recognising too that God created humanity in all its glorious variety can prompt us to commit to breaking down barriers between people and groups in our communities, our nation and our world.

God, we praise you, for you are great and worthy to be praised. We thank you for the beautiful diversity in which you have created us and our world. Help us to embrace that diversity and welcome all.

CHINE MCDONALD

Comfort in the darkness

Rachel Turner writes:

I believe that we all need a theology of God in the dark. From our earliest days, we learn to dislike the dark. There is something about it that unsettles us. Whether it's because we physically cannot see or because our imagination paints our fears on to the blank canvas of the quiet and stillness, we learn that darkness is something to overcome or endure.

This sense of unease can bleed into our feelings about the night. For many of us, night-time can feel like a weird waiting space: the in-between time to put life on pause while we try to achieve unconsciousness, until a new day. Our minds can fight to find rest as we sort through the mental pile of our daily failures and future tasks. Some of us find ourselves gripped with fear from past trauma suffered in the dark, struggling at night to find peace amid our memories. Many of us who are carers or parents face interrupted nights, requiring compassion and energy to deal with the needs of others. Many of us struggle to feel safe in the dark. Night and darkness can feel like a lonely endurance battle.

But it doesn't have to be.

I believe that God is as much himself at night as he is in the daytime. I believe that he is as present in the dark as he is in the light. Scripture is full of stories of who God is and what he does in the dark, at night and in our sleep, and when we begin to see God in the dark, he can transform our nights.

Night-time can be a place where we most often encounter God, where we see him and most feel his closeness. The dark can be a place of deep peace and safety where we rest in the trust of who God is and what he is doing in that exact moment.

I believe this so much that I wrote a book for parents and children to read together – a retelling of biblical stories of the night called *Comfort in the Darkness* (BRF, 2016) – to help children develop a theology of God in the dark. Over the next two weeks, we will be looking at these same stories, because we are all God's children who can learn to look forward to who God is in the night.

God called it good

God set [the stars] in the vault of the sky to give light on the earth, to govern the day and the night, and to separate light from darkness. And God saw that it was good. (NIV)

If we remember nothing else from the creation story, 'Let there be light' tends to be the phrase that sticks with us. It's the declaration of God that starts the creation process. Throughout the following verses, we see God create the sun and form land, oceans and plant life.

But there is one strand of creation that we often overlook – the creation and preservation of darkness.

The whole Bible starts in darkness, 'Darkness was over the surface of the deep' (v. 2). And where was God? Right there, moving and active, hovering over it all. The fullness of him – powerful, peaceful, loving, present – in the dark.

He creates light and sees that it is good. But he doesn't banish the dark – he preserves it. He keeps it. He appoints a space for it. He uses it to create time itself, to mark the passage of life. He creates the sun for the day and the moon for the night, and he calls them both 'good'.

Somehow in our modern lives, we have stopped seeing the night as 'good'. We have stopped looking for God in the darkness. But I believe that he preserved the dark and night for a reason. He has great plans and purposes that he wants to do, especially then.

The night and the dark are gifts from God that he declares as good. What would our nights look like if we anticipated them with joy and the expectation of what God is going to do with us and for us in the night?

God, I believe that you have great things for me in the night. Help me to look for you as darkness falls and anticipate you with peace and hope as you are with me in the dark.

RACHEL TURNER

God is with us in the night

The pillar of cloud was always with them during the day, and the pillar of fire was always with them at night. (NCV)

Do you have a night light in your home? As a child, I remember insisting on having the hallway light left on, with my door open a crack so I could have a stream of light making me feel safe.

God seems to know our need to feel safe in the dark. When the Israelites were finally leaving Egypt, he showed himself to them in a pillar of cloud. This pillar directed them and showed them where and when to go. It guided them. It reminded them that God was with them and taking care of them. But God knew that his people didn't just need reminders in the day; they also needed a reminder at night. So he made his massive pillar of cloud glow at night as if it were on fire: a huge light in the darkness to show his children that he was with them in the night. The ultimate night light! Its purpose was not to fight the darkness, but to show his children where he was in the midst of it.

Many of us can struggle to find God in the night. The quiet solitude (or endless chaos, depending on your family) can feel isolating and lonely. But God is there. He is close, never sleeping, ever present and ready to engage with us.

God provided the Israelites with a tangible statement of his presence to grow their confidence in him. We don't usually have a supernatural glowing pillar of fire to remind us at night, but God is just as present in our nights as he was then. How would our nights change if we felt as sure of God's closeness at night?

If a tangible reminder would help you, ask God what a small reminder could be for you: a framed verse, a bookmark, a song to listen to at bedtime, a candle or anything else creative you think would help.

RACHEL TURNER

God provides in the night

The Lord said to Moses, 'I have heard the grumblings of the people of Israel. So tell them, "At twilight you will eat meat, and every morning you will eat all the bread you want. Then you will know I am the Lord your God."' (NCV)

Forty-five days into their retreat from slavery, the Israelites were nervous. Depending on the translation you are reading, the author describes them as 'grumbling' or 'complaining' against God about their food provisions. The Israelites were unhappy, stressed in the barren desert they were trudging through, and asking themselves if it really was so bad back in Egypt, in slavery.

Thousands of people were crammed together, being led to a place they had never been before, having left everything behind. Water was scarce. Food was running out. If it were me, I'd be slightly panicking too.

Often my worries come out at night. When I lay down and try to sleep, the fears and stresses of the future can whirl in my mind. Where will I find the money for the MOT for the car? How can I get access to the medication the pharmacy can't seem to find? Will my child break through his fear about something or other? Some needs may be exaggerated, while others are very real and pressing, with large consequences if they don't get sorted. I could spend all night churning in my stress and worry.

In this passage, God does something remarkable. He tells the people to sleep and that when they wake up, his provision for their needs will be there. He promises them that while they are sleeping, he will sort it out. While they are unconscious, he will provide.

God never tires; he never stops. He works on our behalf through the night. What would our nights look like if we deliberately and consciously handed over all our cares and worries to God, trusting him to work on our behalf as we sleep? What would it be like to wake up with our first thought being, 'What was God doing last night?'

Tonight, as you get into bed, tell God bluntly and honestly what is pressing on your heart. Tell him openly what needs you have. Then thank him for what he is going to do while you are sleeping.

RACHEL TURNER

God speaks in the night

The Lord came and stood there and called as he had before, 'Samuel, Samuel!' Samuel said, 'Speak, Lord. I am your servant and I am listening.' (NCV)

While this story centres on a child's first encounter with God, I love what it reveals to us about how God communicates to us.

First, I love how he chooses to talk to Samuel in the middle of the night – not when Samuel is alert and awake, at his best or his holiest, but when he is alone, quiet and very sleepy. There is something about the night that creates a space for God to communicate, something about our stillness or openness that invites a moment with God. God doesn't think – 'Oh, she brushed her teeth; I'll just wait for tomorrow.' He instead draws close and speaks. The dark places of the night can be beautiful places of encounter with God.

Second, I love how God doesn't give up. Over and over, he called Samuel. I believe that God was so faithful that he would have kept calling to Samuel until he understood. How many nights have I tossed and turned, wanting to know God's messages to me, but struggled to know if it was him? This story gives me peace that God will keep whispering until my heart knows what he is saying and can respond.

Third, I love how God started the conversation. It wasn't Samuel begging God to speak or beating down the doors of heaven with his prayers. God himself wanted to share with Samuel. He waited until the night when Samuel was ready and then he spoke.

As we lie down each night, let us be aware of the God who communicates. As the stillness of the dark wraps around us, let us be ready to respond to the God who speaks at night, seeking us out, faithfully communicating until we can know him and respond.

God, thank you that the quiet places of the night are times when we can meet with you. Please make my nights a time of heart-to-heart communication with you.

RACHEL TURNER

God brings songs in the night

By day the Lord directs his love, at night his song is with me – a prayer to the God of my life. (NIV)

The Bible is full of songs, and people sing in the Bible quite a lot. There are over 180 songs recorded in scripture. The book of Psalms has 150 of them, but that leaves around 35 scattered through the other books: songs of praise, celebration, worship and declaration. It can be hard sometimes to connect with them as songs, as all we have are the lyrics, but it is clear: God is a God of songs.

In today's reading, we are reading the lyrics of a song. And in the middle of this song, the writer declares that God's song shows up at night. Night, of course, isn't the only time songs occur in our lives, but I love that the writer of this song felt it important to highlight the night as a time and place of God's song.

Songs allow us to tap into emotions and feelings that we find hard to express in other ways. They function as memory holders and truth declarers. Songs help us connect with God and remind us of his truth.

Some of my earliest memories are of lying in bed and singing to God; of songs popping in my head and me singing out loud to him. My husband tells me that during most of his teenage years, he couldn't sleep unless he played worship music. A friend of mine tells me that often when she is chatting to God in bed about her worries, a worship song will begin niggling in her brain, easing her heart and lifting her eyes to God.

God often brings his song in the night, to be with us, to draw us into connection with him. What would our nights be like if we were open to what songs he is bringing?

God, as I lay down tonight, fill my heart and mind with your songs. As I rest and fall asleep, bring to my mind songs that speak of you.

RACHEL TURNER

God rescues us at night

At the first light of dawn, the king got up and hurried to the lions' den. (NIV)

Throughout scripture, we see God rescuing people from a vast array of perils, including hostile armies, drowning, unjust imprisonment, assassination attempts, shipwrecks, stoning and, in this case, a horrible death being eaten by lions. Many of these instances happened at night. When others slept, God moved. When others sat in fear, he acted.

It can bring us enormous comfort to cry out to the God who rescues, 'Rescue me now, God!' I remember repeating this phrase over and over to God through a haze of pain during my time with cancer. There is something in us that cries out to the God who never sleeps, to lift us from the pit of fear and danger and rescue us. And often he does.

There will be others of us who struggle with this passage, because there have been times when we needed a rescuer and he seemingly didn't come. It might have been a time in our childhood or a more recent experience; it might have been ourselves or someone we love who needed the miracle of rescue. Either way, it appears that God didn't show up. I cannot offer you a reason. I cannot explain away why he didn't do what you so wanted him to do. The Bible shares stories like yours as well, of people who weren't rescued and how they responded, where God was and what he was doing. The writers of psalms often lament, rant and praise in the midst of it all. Yet over and over, we are reminded that God is the rescuer, and he often moves at night when we least expect it.

God, raise in us the hope of you, our rescuer. Rescue us now from dangers we face, whether we know of them or not. Meet with us in our pain, confusion or fear, and be our rescuer tonight.

RACHEL TURNER

God sends messages to us in the night

'Where is the one who has been born king of the Jews? We saw his star when it rose and have come to worship him.' (NIV)

I have always been fascinated by the star that led the Magi to Jesus after he was born. Was it in fact three planets aligning and just looking like a bright star? Or was it a new star that God especially created for the purpose? Did it really move? If so, was it more like a UFO light in the sky than an actual star? Did it disappear after the Magi found Jesus, or is it still in the sky today and I just don't know which one it is? Given how many stars are in the sky, how is it possible the Magi could confidently identify a new one? I am amazed at how God wove this sign into the night sky for people to find and follow to Jesus.

But I'm also struck by its specialness. It was a sign that someone could only find in the dark – in the darkest dark. I lived in London for a while, and I can tell you that stargazing there isn't easy. The never-ending light from the city makes it almost impossible to see the stars clearly. But if I got out of the city, to the countryside, far from towns or cities on a clear moonless night, then the sky was breathtaking, more stars than I could ever count covering the sky. The darker it was around me, the more clearly I could see the stars.

God is not limited by time. He appointed day and night and has plans and purposes for both of them. And apparently some messages from him can only be perceived at night.

I wonder: what truths are waiting to be revealed during our nights with God? What does he want to show us that he has held back to show us at night?

God, we are ready for what you want to show us tonight. Train our eyes and hearts to be aware of what you are saying and doing, that we might not miss any of your night-time messages.

RACHEL TURNER

God listens to us at night

Very early in the morning, while it was still dark, Jesus got up, left the house and went off to a solitary place, where he prayed. (NIV)

This story always makes me laugh. Jesus was just starting his ministry. He didn't yet have all of his twelve disciples. They were all sleeping on the floor at Simon's mother-in-law's house at the start of their journey together. As they woke up in the early morning, Jesus' disciples must have looked around and discovered in horror that the man they were supposed to be 'following' had left. Was he lost? Did he leave to go to another town without telling them? They decided to run around looking for Jesus, until finally they found him. He evidently explained to them that he had gone off to pray, and then he unfolded the next strategy to launch his ministry.

This would not be the last time Jesus headed off on his own overnight. Throughout his ministry, Jesus would retreat for some overnight time alone with God.

God is always listening to us, always ready to hear when we want to share our thoughts and feelings with him. But even Jesus felt drawn to connect with God in prayer in the night. From his overnights on the hills of Galilee to his final night of intercession in the garden of Gethsemane, Jesus sought God out at night.

Some of my most precious times with God have been in the night. There are times when I'm too tired to try to say things correctly, when emotion is raw or when the peace of my surroundings enables me to speak the truth of my heart to God. Night offers us opportunities to hold nothing back in our communication with God, to put down all sense of performing for God and meet with him in the seclusion of the night.

Take some time tonight to tell God about your worries and fears or to chat to him about your children or colleague. Don't worry about what you say; simply share all of what is in you with him.

RACHEL TURNER

God responds to our prayers at night

So Peter was kept in prison, but the church was earnestly praying to God for him. (NIV)

I talked with a woman once who described to me her experience of prayer at night: 'It's as if I'm leaving a long voicemail message for God. I feel like I've communicated, but I'm left with that empty wondering feeling of hoping he gets the message and does something about it. I hope, but I've never quite sure.'

Peter's friends in this passage appear to have had a similar experience. King Herod was at the time killing Christians and in the recent past had executed one of Jesus' twelve disciples. Due to the wild popularity of that action, Herod then arrested Peter, with, we assume, the same purpose. Peter's friends were desperate. They gathered together to pray for God to do a miracle. While Peter slept and his friends prayed, God miraculously released Peter. And yet when he showed up at their door, they didn't believe it. When Rhoda, the servant, came back to tell them that Peter was at the door, they told her she was out of her mind. They were praying, and yet they were unsure that God would do anything.

God moves in response to our prayers. Night-time isn't a time when we passively leave messages, hoping for God to pick them up at a time convenient to him and maybe do something about. He responds as we ask. He is active through the night. While I see this passage as a call to pray for others at night, I'm also encouraged that God is moving in response to other people's prayers while I sleep. While Peter slept, God was preparing for his release. While the night moved on, God heard the prayers of his people and responded. Are we bold enough to share with others what we need prayer for?

Take a moment to pray for others you know who need God to work on their behalf tonight. Thank God for those who pray for you, and rest peacefully knowing that God is active while you sleep.

RACHEL TURNER

God sees us in the night

Where can I go to get away from your Spirit? Where can I run from you? If I go up to the heavens, you are there. If I lie down in the grave, you are there. (NCV)

Many scholars believe that David (of David and Goliath fame) wrote this song when he was hiding in caves as he was being hunted by King Saul. He was fearful, confused and worried. And yet, he lifted his eyes and invited God in.

There are many character flaws in my life that I am working on. One of those flaws is how I respond to my many mistakes or failings. When I mess up, especially when dealing with other people, my first instinct is to run away and hide, never to have to speak to that person again and avoid facing the agony of worrying that others think less of me. Even though it is my failure, I instantly slam up walls in my heart to protect myself from their potential negative response. I hide.

This psalm, this song of David's, calls us to do the opposite. He flings his heart open to God and shouts to him, 'I can hide nothing from you. Search every bit of me.' Darkness cannot hide us from God's knowledge of our minds, hearts and souls. So rather than seek to hide and to raise internal walls to separate him from God, David instead says to God, 'Know me.' In his darkest place of fear, in the desert of his heart, in the darkest night, David chooses to be known by God.

His boldness inspires me to spend time in my night, in the dark, willing to say, 'Know me, God, in all of my sin, imperfection, hopes, dreams and fears. Search my heart. Forgive my sins. Bring your comfort, guidance and truth to the places I want to hide. Let there be nothing held back between us.'

What a beautiful opportunity we have each night to be known by God.

God, search my heart and know me fully. I hold nothing back from you. See the fullness of me, the good and the bad. Forgive me for anything that gets in between you and me.

RACHEL TURNER

God enables us to rest

Truly my soul finds rest in God. (NIV)

There are times when I have felt like I am in a battle for sleep. Whether it's my troubled mind or just the menopause making my nights broken and unrestful, I can feel as if my peace has been stolen from me. I'm often in awe at how important sleep is to our bodies, how God created us to need sleep. In our sleep, memories are formed, toxins in our brains are removed, experiences are processed, repairs are made and bodies are restored. When our sleep gets disrupted, through fear or circumstance, there is a cost to us.

God is the God of sleep. We hear of multiple stories in scripture of God putting people into deep sleep, like Adam and Abraham. We read repeatedly of God encountering people in their dreams, giving them gifts, wisdom and guidance. Joseph, the wise men, Solomon, Paul – the list goes on of people who met with God in their dreams.

Sleep is a gift from God, and he cares about it. Do you remember falling asleep feeling safe as a child? Whether it was with your parents, grandparents, carers or teachers, you may have a memory of falling asleep next to an adult who made you feel totally safe and able to truly rest because that safe adult was guarding you.

In this passage, God declares that he is that safety for us each night. He is the one able to protect us, able to be awake when we aren't and able to surround us with his love and protection. When I crawl into bed, I picture God sitting next to me. I remind myself of this verse and picture myself so close that I sleep in his shadow.

Where do you picture God is when you close your eyes to sleep?

God, I thank you that you are my refuge and my strength. I want to sleep next to you, filled with trust in you. Help me find peace and rest tonight with you.
RACHEL TURNER

God joins us in the dark to lead us through

With a loud cry, Jesus breathed his last. (NIV)

It may seem odd to talk about the crucifixion of Jesus in a series about the night and darkness. Scripture is clear that Jesus was executed during the day. But in the middle of this particular day, darkness intruded. In the passage we read today, darkness came over the whole land for a period of three hours leading up to Jesus' death, as if nature itself was responding to the importance of what was about to happen.

As Jesus died on the cross, he entered into the darkness for us. He bore the weight of all we have kept on our hearts, all the sin we clung to, all the pain and hurt and anger we have, and chose to pay the ultimate price to free us. He came into the dark places to be with us.

In that time of darkness, our freedom was gained.

That's why there is no place he cannot be with us. There is no place of our heart he cannot go. There is no sin too great, fear so strong or problem so complex that he cannot bring freedom. We need not be afraid of the dark, because God has provided for us in all circumstances and walks straight into them to be with us through it all.

What are the places of darkness in our lives where we feel lonely? What are the times of struggle when we feel hopeless and stuck? What do we see in the lives of our family and friends that make us despair with the darkness we see? May we learn to grab on to the God who stands with us in the dark to bring safety, comfort and freedom – that in all times we may live to the fullness of all he has for us.

Thank you, God, that you are the same in all circumstances and that nothing holds you back. Teach me how to find you when I feel hopeless, lonely or stuck, that together with your freedom we may walk through it.

RACHEL TURNER

God speaks truth in the night

But after he had considered this, an angel of the Lord appeared to him in a dream and said, 'Joseph son of David, do not be afraid to take Mary home as your wife, because what is conceived in her is from the Holy Spirit.' (NIV)

When Joseph lay down to sleep that night, he could have been feeling any number of emotions: disappointment, betrayal, worry, anger, humiliation. He felt that he understood the situation and had decided what to do about it. His fiancée was pregnant, and it wasn't by him. He had decided to quietly break their engagement. As he fell asleep that night, God intervened. God gave him a dream and spoke truth to him.

I find it interesting that he wasn't looking for that from God. We have no record of him tossing and turning, begging God for answers. It appears that God simply stepped in to give him truth where he was lacking it.

There are so many circumstances in life where I lack information, where I may have got the wrong end of the stick or where I have misinterpreted people's actions or words or been nursing hurt when none was intended. We all are such fragile beings, limited in our understanding to what is in front of us. But God is so much bigger.

This child God speaks about to Joseph is Jesus, who promises to us that the Holy Spirit will 'guide you into all the truth' (John 16:13).

I need that from God. I need him to intervene in my life and show me the truth of the situations I find myself in. When we open ourselves to seeing our lives from his perspective, everything can change. Joseph woke up and, armed with the truth, married Mary and got to have the incredible experience of serving as a father to God's Son.

As we lay down to sleep each night, let us lay open our lives to God and invite him to review our days with us and bring his truth into them.

God, tonight as I lie in bed, I invite you to bring your truth into my life. Show me where I am wrong, where I am not seeing as you see. I want to live out of the truth.

RACHEL TURNER

God guides us in the night

During the night Paul had a vision of a man of Macedonia standing and begging him, 'Come over to Macedonia and help us.' (NIV)

Poor Paul and his companions had been confused for quite a while. They wanted to go where God wanted, but they kept missing the mark. They headed in one direction, but it appeared that it was the wrong way to go. So they tried another destination, but that didn't seem right either. Eventually they landed at Troas, still seeking where God was leading. As they lit their fires and huddled in for the night, God finally dropped in Paul's mind where he wanted them to go. And they could get a boat straight there from the port where they happened to be!

We all can feel a bit lost sometimes, looking for guidance from God about what to do next. Whether it's about a family situation, a job opportunity or a major life change we are considering, we often want clear direction from God.

The Bible is full of stories of God guiding people in the night – there are five examples just within the story of Jesus' birth and early few years!

What situations are you facing where you need God's guidance? He is a God who promises to guide us, and night-time is a wonderful time when he may do it.

As we move forward, let's remember that God is in the night-time too, and he called night 'good'. He is with us in the night. He provides for us, speaks to us and brings his songs to us. He rescues us, brings us messages and listens as we pour out our hearts to him. He sees our hearts, responds to our prayers and gives us rest. He joins us in the dark places of our lives and speaks truth to us, guiding us through and giving us freedom.

May the night, darkness and sleep be a blessed and beautiful time with our Father each and every night.

RACHEL TURNER

Rich towards God: money and treasure

Sheila Jacobs writes:

Many of us will be familiar with the parable found in Luke 12 of the man who built big barns and hoarded his wealth, deciding to take life easy at last – only to find that his planning was all for nothing, because God had different ideas. Actually, God calls him a 'fool' (v. 20, NIV). Who will get the rich man's wealth once he is dead? He has spent his precious life focusing on the wrong thing – what a waste! Jesus concludes his sobering story by saying that this is how it is for people who aren't 'rich towards God' (v. 21).

But what does it mean to be 'rich towards God'? Perhaps you are thinking about the collection plate being passed round the congregation on Sunday mornings. Does it just mean that God expects us to be financially generous towards the church and good causes? That we should give tithes and offerings regularly? Is it all about money and possessions, and how we shouldn't hoard them but give them away? Or is there more to it than that?

I think there's a whole lot more to it. You see, money is a good thermometer: it tells us all about our spiritual temperature. My attitude towards money and possessions says a great deal about my heart. It tells me a lot about my faith. It shows me where I ultimately put my trust – whatever I might tell others. In fact, reviewing my attitude towards material stuff challenges me massively on what I truly believe… what the 'treasure' of my heart and life really is.

Once we start thinking about money and possessions, it can lead us to reflect upon what we really value. And that may be quite a wake-up call for some of us.

In Luke 18:22, Jesus spoke about having 'treasure in heaven'. The thought of treasure conjures up in my mind a big box overflowing with gems, but that's the result of watching too much TV when I was younger! Real treasure means much more than what I might wear on my finger or around my neck.

So let's explore together what it means to be rich towards God and think about what true treasure – heavenly treasure – really looks like. I hope you will be blessed, encouraged and challenged.

Treasure... in heaven

When Jesus heard this, he said to him, 'You still lack one thing. Sell everything you have and give to the poor, and you will have treasure in heaven. Then come, follow me.' (NIV)

In this passage we read that a man – a 'ruler' – asks Jesus what he has to do to have eternal life. Jesus tells him to keep the commandments – which the ruler says he has done. Jesus replies that he still lacks something: the man must give away all that he owns and 'follow me'. If he does this, he'll have 'treasure in heaven'. The ruler just can't do it. And Jesus points out to his followers how difficult it is for the rich to enter God's kingdom. Why is that? Could it be because it is so hard to let go of wealth, once we have it – the security, the status, the power that it brings?

How much am I like the rich ruler? I wouldn't term myself 'rich', although living in the western world, comparatively I am. Yes, I'm a follower of Jesus, but I also like my comfort: my home, my garden, my car... so how authentic am I being when I sing songs about Jesus being all I need?

When I was younger, long-term sickness meant my great dreams of owning a beautiful cottage (plus luxury kitchen) all crashed into the dust. I couldn't earn money or do anything much. But it was at that time that I experienced the presence of Jesus so closely I could almost reach out and touch him.

Thanks to God, my health was restored, and I began to get back into the swing of 'ordinary' life. But I wonder: do I still see my treasure as being solely in heaven, as I did when I felt I had nothing to cling to on this earth? Isn't treasure less about some*thing* and more about some*one*?

How do you define 'treasure'? Is treasure for you something that is here and now, or is it above?

SHEILA JACOBS

God *and*...?

Then [Jesus] said to them, 'Watch out! Be on your guard against all kinds of greed; life does not consist in an abundance of possessions.' (NIV)

It's so hard, in this culture, where TV promotes the latest must-have gadgets as essential to our lives, to stand back and review what we are watching and how it is affecting our beliefs and goals.

It's great to be blessed with good things, but when (and if) we pray for material wealth, I wonder what our motives really are. Is our longed-for abundance to help others? To expand the kingdom? We need to be careful of so-called 'prosperity gospel' thinking and to exercise discernment. Sometimes my own prayers reflect this kind of sentiment: 'I can only be really happy, God, if I have such-and-such.' Surely that's an outlook that belongs to my old life, before I met Jesus. Perhaps I need to reflect on my longings and see what they say about my heart attitude. Is God all I need? Or is it 'God *and*…'?

My mother has dementia, as well as Parkinson's disease and other health complications. Yet when I went to see her in the care home recently, lying there in her little bedroom, she told me that she felt the presence of Jesus, and added, 'It gives me joy.' There was such a sense of peace around her at that moment. I left asking myself, 'What's *rich*, really?'

Where's my heart? Where's my treasure? Is it in my bank balance, my home – or in heaven? Is a closer walk with Jesus what I am truly longing for? Or does that desire vie with the longing for a new car, new computer, new phone, new (fill in the blank)? If we get our sights right, everything else will drop into place (Matthew 6:33). Maybe it won't be quite the life we envisaged; but then, we're part of a bigger picture – a picture we can't see.

Reflect on Jesus' words, 'Life does not consist in an abundance of possessions.' What might he be saying to you? How will you respond?

SHEILA JACOBS

Cheerfully giving

'God said to him, "You fool! This very night your life will be demanded from you. Then who will get what you have prepared for yourself?" This is how it will be with whoever stores up things for themselves but is not rich towards God.' (NIV)

I find the story of Ebenzer Scrooge really interesting – so interesting that I recently wrote a book based on *A Christmas Carol*. Scrooge loved money. It was his security. He trusted it. He hoarded it. He didn't share it, or himself, with anyone. And he was miserable.

2 Corinthians 9:7 tells us that 'God loves a cheerful giver', but it doesn't stipulate how much we are meant to place on the plate/in the bag that's passed around on Sundays at church. However, it does tell us something of our heart attitude – we are to give happily, 'not reluctantly or under compulsion'. If we're clenching our teeth as we part with some of our hard-earned cash, there may be a problem!

Some Christians think it is a good idea to set aside a portion of their income, called a 'tithe', or 'tenth'. The teaching stems from the Old Testament law, but even before that, we read that Abram (later Abraham) gave a tenth of all he had to the king of Salem (Genesis 14:20). Malachi 3:8–10 speaks of people robbing God of the tithe and of offerings, and it seems that God sets a test that if the people give their tenth, he will bless in abundance. 'It is the Lord's blessing that makes a person rich' (Proverbs 10:22, GW). But does that always mean materially wealthy?

Giving a tenth of our income is a good discipline when it comes to giving, although some don't see a tenth as binding in the New Testament. I think God blesses us when we are generous towards him in attitude – which will include how we choose to share our material goods. After all, he is generous and we, his children, should be like him.

What are some of the non-material riches God might bless us with? Peace? Time with people we love? How do you think he might be asking you to be richer towards him today?

SHEILA JACOBS

Where your treasure is...

'Sell your possessions and give to the poor. Provide purses for yourselves that will not wear out, a treasure in heaven that will never fail, where no thief comes near and no moth destroys. For where your treasure is, there your heart will be also.' (NIV)

It's very easy to slide into a position where we trust in money and 'things' rather than trust in God. We may *say* we trust him, but do we?

I don't think God asks everyone to sell everything they own and give it away – and we have to be practical, in that there are always bills to be paid, and if we have families they need to be provided for. So we should try to be responsible. But how do we do this without letting our hearts become ensnared by the 'security' promised by wealth? Ultimately, where is our security truly to be found?

It's where our hearts are that matters. If we are working for, aiming for and storing up material possessions, we may not want to leave them. 1 Timothy 6:7 tells us: 'For we brought nothing into the world, and we can take nothing out of it.' And in Matthew 16:26, Jesus warns us not to gain the world at the expense of our soul.

If we can thank God for material provision, but hold on to it lightly, it will be one of his blessings not 'our treasure' – it will not possess our heart. If our treasure is in and with God, we can never lose it. It will be kept in heaven for us, a beautiful inheritance – much more than the world can give us (1 Peter 1:4).

Sometimes I think I live as if this world is all there is. What about you? We need to remember that we are just passing through, pilgrims, journeying in this life and heading for eternity. We need to invest in our true future.

Our attitude to possessions tells us what we truly believe. Actions always show what's really in the heart.

Lord, thank you that I have an inheritance in heaven: one that can never be taken from me. Thank you, Jesus, that you made this possible.

SHEILA JACOBS

Serving God

'No one can serve two masters. Either you will hate the one and love the other, or you will be devoted to the one and despise the other. You cannot serve both God and Money.' (NIV)

Jesus said we can't serve God and money, but many of us try to. I'm not really talking about those of us who work long and tiring hours and then find we haven't got the time or energy to meet with other Christians/do church – although if this describes you, you may feel you need to review what's happening in your life. When I first became a Christian, I tended to view my secular job as something apart from my Christian walk. Years of illness and not being able to work changed my ideas: whether working or not, if we're disciples, then being present with him is the most important thing.

In whatever way we live our lives, whether at work, at home, taking care of family, in unemployment, in the quietness of solitude, or if we are older and retired, we can be living wholeheartedly for Jesus.

If we are working, we need to work hard not just to pay the bills but because it gives glory to God (Colossians 3:23). However, if we find ourselves relentlessly obsessing over work or money, then we perhaps need to consider changes we could make in our lifestyle.

So let's think about perspectives. Is our life about money, status, satisfaction? Or are we aware of, and consequently serving, God as we carry out our daily tasks?

If we worship wealth, we are in danger of becoming hardened to the things of God. We may believe that everything we possess has been the result of *our* doing, rather than being from God (Proverbs 10:22a). Isaiah 26:12 says: 'All that we have accomplished you [God] have done for us.' Sometimes we forget that it is God who gives us the strength and ability, and the health, to live out our daily lives.

Review your day-to-day life. Is God a very real part of it? Be honest! Does your lifestyle reveal your 'devotion' to him? Or are you serving two (or more) masters?

SHEILA JACOBS

True treasure

'Again, the kingdom of heaven is like a merchant looking for fine
pearls. When he found one of great value, he went away and sold
everything he had and bought it.' (NIV)

What (or who) do you value most in the world? Peace? Freedom? Health?
Someone you love? A pet? Holidays? Your home? Your job? Or is it your
salvation?

The parables of the hidden treasure and the pearl are one and the same
thing. They're stories Jesus told about finding something of such value
that it turns your world upside down, something so valuable you will risk
everything else to gain, or keep, the thing you have found.

When I surrendered my life to Jesus, I was 25 years old. I'd been hearing
his call for several years but had managed to resist, until I encountered a
series of difficulties. I'd always believed in God and known Jesus was my
Saviour, but I hadn't fully submitted to him as Lord. I needed to know that
he was *real*. I discovered he was, and it changed everything. But *letting*
Jesus be Lord of my life is a daily choice.

I've had to make some serious life adjustments to authentically follow Christ. My wants and my ambitions often battle to get back on the
throne of my life. But I found something that is far more precious to me
than anything else – Jesus. To me, it's about maintaining that relationship
with him, not doing religious stuff. His presence is true treasure. When
we realise what he did for us on the cross, making it possible for us to be
restored into relationship with God, at such a huge price, we must surely
admit that nothing compares to this – the richness that can be found in his
company, the depth of security, knowing that he is love and that he loves
us as unique individuals.

God calls us to a deeper relationship with him, one that will impact us
and the world around us.

What do you value most in the world? How tight a hold does it have on you?
Think about it.

SHEILA JACOBS

Good stewards

What is more, I consider everything a loss because of the surpassing worth of knowing Christ Jesus my Lord, for whose sake I have lost all things. I consider them garbage, that I may gain Christ and be found in him, not having a righteousness of my own. (NIV)

Of all the people in the world, the apostle Paul had the most to boast about when it came to legalistic righteousness. Yet he said that he considered everything 'garbage' when compared with knowing Christ. His priorities had radically shifted on realising that Christ is 'our righteousness, holiness and redemption' (1 Corinthians 1:30).

So power, wealth, all the trappings of a lavish lifestyle, even outwardly religious works – anything we can gain in this world – when compared with Jesus and what he has done for us, it's trash! And there is a lost world, people you know who don't yet see where true treasure can be found.

If God has blessed us financially, we are wise if we consider how we can use it to help further the gospel, to invite people to know the God who loves them and to share with those who are in all kinds of need. If we find it hard to 'let go' as and when God asks us to give, it is perhaps time to pray that God will help us. Let's not hold on too tightly to what we have in this world, because one day it won't be ours anymore. We are merely stewards. Let's make sure we are good ones and that our money and possessions have eternal significance.

In Luke 16, Jesus interestingly talks about 'true riches' (v. 11). He says if we can't be trusted with 'worldly wealth', how can we be trusted with the riches that are of much greater value? If we haven't been good stewards of earthly, temporal things, how can we be trusted with those that are eternal? Holding on lightly means we are free to pick up other things that God may want to give – to us, in us and through us.

Are you a good steward of what God has given you? How might he be asking you to be an ever-better steward of all that you have?

SHEILA JACOBS

Comfortable living

Command those who are rich in this present world not to... put their hope in wealth... Command them to do good... In this way they will lay up treasure for themselves... so that they may take hold of the life that is truly life. (NIV)

We've been considering what it means to be rich towards God, and I hope we are beginning to see that it's about aligning our sights. Heavenly treasure can't be reviewed on a bank statement. Loving worldly stuff leads nowhere good; indeed, the 'deceitfulness of wealth' (Mark 4:19) can potentially choke our authentic Christian walk and witness. It can lead us away from the life of discipleship, and, rather than bringing us happiness and comfort, Paul says it will bring us grief (v. 10).

You simply can't 'take it with you', so why focus on such a temporary thing? Heavenly treasure is something far better. It's the life that Paul exhorts Timothy to tell his congregation about: 'the life that is truly life'.

Jesus, 'the life', came to set us free (John 14:6; 8:36). What does this freedom mean? Jesus bought us freedom *on the inside*. We don't need to be slaves to money, things or status anymore. We can be free to be the people God calls us to be – free to live life as he wants us to live it.

The disciples left all they had to follow Jesus (Matthew 19:27). Maybe, for some of us, following him *will* mean financial recalibrations and perhaps a complete change of lifestyle and values. Seeing our money as God's gift to us may help – and remembering that God is our provider. James 1:17 tells us that 'every good and perfect gift is from above', and James goes on to say that our faith needs to be one of deeds as well as words (James 2:16–17). If we have the means to do good, and don't do it, that's sin (James 4:17). The book of James is a great read if you'd like to be challenged about 'comfortable' living!

Is there an area where God may be asking you to change a habit or lifestyle, so that you can 'take hold of the life that is truly life'?

SHEILA JACOBS

The treasure of all treasures

My goal is that they may be encouraged… and united… so that they may have the full riches of complete understanding, in order that they may know the mystery of God, namely, Christ, in whom are hidden all the treasures of wisdom and knowledge. (NIV)

All wisdom and knowledge is found in Christ – heavenly treasure, which the world cannot buy. When people ask me why I believe in Jesus, I often point them to the gospel of John. There, they will be able to consider what Jesus said about himself.

Jesus claimed, 'I am the way and the truth and the life. No one comes to the Father except through me' (John 14:6). He is the only way to God (Acts 4:12). He is God in the flesh (Colossians 2:9; Hebrews 1:3). Only a human could pay the price for humankind's sin. Only God could live a perfect life and then lay it down on behalf of others. It's a sacrifice of eternal proportions.

When we really see that all the fullness of God lives in Jesus, the crucified and risen Saviour, and we surrender ourselves to him, we begin a different kind of life: one lived in and by the power of the Spirit (John 3:3) and one that can be rich towards God in the everyday, enjoying his presence, reading his word, listening to him, praising him, thanking him, interceding for others and using God's gifts for everlasting purposes – for the good of others who don't yet know him, as well as for the good of people who do.

So the treasure of all treasures is found in Christ. In this world, we all seem to live at a faster pace than ever before. It can be helpful, therefore, to take time out just to focus again on Jesus. Let's not allow the pressures of life to squeeze the reality of this treasure to the margins of our existence, so that we finish up giving him lip service in a life that is little different from those who don't know him.

Lord, help me to take time away from all the busyness of my life and turn my eyes again to you, and you alone. Thank you for all that you have done for me.
SHEILA JACOBS

Jars of clay

But we have this treasure in jars of clay to show that this all-surpassing power is from God and not from us. (NIV)

Have you ever been so hard-pressed that you didn't think you'd survive? Perhaps it was because of an illness, financial difficulties or relationship problems. Maybe you have suffered some kind of loss because of your faith in Jesus. Isn't it a comfort to know that you're a jar of clay and that the light which burns within you, so much brighter and stronger than your circumstances, is God himself?

When we come to Christ, he gives us his Holy Spirit to live inside us and to give us the power to live a new life: a life pleasing to God. All our anxious striving can't make us right with God. When we realise this, we acknowledge our need for a Saviour. But how many of us then try to 'work for God' in our own strength, forgetting the treasure we have inside us? I did, until I became ill and couldn't 'work for God'. Then I understood that God wanted to do *his* work in and through me!

How great is the glory given to God when he is able to show himself working in us, the clay jars that somehow let the light shine through them! When whatever we are facing is beyond our ability to cope with, how wonderful it is to know that someone stronger is with us – and in us (Philippians 4:13). What a witness to a lost world, if we respond out of the grace and peace of God when we find ourselves in tough situations. Do you need to rely on that inner strength of God today? Maybe you need to spend time with him, being real about your circumstances.

Christ, in us, 'the hope of glory' (Colossians 1:27), is the true treasure: the treasure that lives in us!

We often pray to a God 'out there' and forget he is 'in us' too. How might your becoming more aware of the Spirit living in you affect the way you live your life – and impact those around you?

SHEILA JACOBS

Treasured possession

And the Lord has declared this day that you are his people, his treasured possession as he promised, and that you are to keep all his commands. (NIV)

What do you think when you look in the mirror? Do negative words flood into your mind? Words people have spoken over you – perhaps many years ago?

The passage above and others speak of Israel as being God's 'treasured possession'. Under the new covenant, we no longer need to rely on the law to make us right with God. We now have the sacrifice of Jesus' own blood that has brought us into right relationship with God. When we receive Jesus and believe in him, we become God's 'children' (John 1:12–13). We are loved. We are valued. We are his treasured possession.

Becoming rich towards God, as we have been considering, is about the way we live. It's about our relationship with Jesus. This will affect everything we do and all that we are. Once we can grasp how much we are loved – not just acknowledging it in our minds but actually *knowing* it in our hearts – we should find our hands letting go of the things of this world, being raised instead to heaven in praise. That's when faith becomes reality, rather than just a word – when it becomes a lifestyle, rather than an add-on. It's when we begin to stop measuring ourselves by the standard of a world which tells us that we are only worth what we have in the bank. Money and possessions aren't what make us truly rich. Spending time with God, getting to know him, realising how much he loves us and those around us, and letting the divine company we keep change our view and attitude are all a part of being rich towards him.

Ask Jesus to show you, through his word and through his Spirit, how much of a 'treasure' you are!

Come, Holy Spirit. Fill me till I am overflowing with your love.

SHEILA JACOBS

The key

[God] will be the sure foundation for your times, a rich store of salvation and wisdom and knowledge; the fear of the Lord is the key to this treasure. (NIV)

Keys to treasure sound so exciting. So when we read here that the key to the 'rich store of salvation and wisdom and knowledge' is 'fear', how do you react? Of course, it isn't just a general fear – it's specific: the 'fear of the Lord'.

In my experience, there are people who think that God is 'up there somewhere', just waiting for us to get it wrong. That might even have been your idea of God before you came to know Jesus. Dare I ask – is it still your view now, even a little bit?

God is the righteous 'Judge of all the earth' (Genesis 18:25). Sin – the wrong things we say and do and even the way we are – has separated us from our holy God, and there will be judgement (Hebrews 9:27). But sin has been judged in Jesus, and that's the good news of the gospel. Fear of judgement can drive us to our knees in repentance. But there we will find forgiveness and love – and 'perfect love drives out fear' (1 John 4:18). When we know Jesus, fear of punishment is replaced with thankfulness that he has taken what we deserve and bought us life.

So the fear of God becomes an awed reverence for the all-powerful, per-fect God who loves us so much he doesn't want us to face eternal separation from him and has done something about it when we couldn't (John 3:16). Recognising who he is and what he has done, that he has provided a way for us to be restored before we even knew we needed help, should bring a flow of gratitude and expectation – and a desire to be rich towards him in every way.

What incredible love. Treasure indeed!

Are you afraid of God, or do you have a healthy awe of him? Ask Jesus for a deeper revelation of who he is and how much he loves you. How might this impact your life?

SHEILA JACOBS

Treasure in darkness

'I will give you hidden treasures, riches stored in secret places, so that you may know that I am the Lord, the God of Israel, who summons you by name.' (NIV)

These are words originally written to a pagan king, but verse 3 quoted above is compelling because it speaks to us of discovering treasure in places we may not expect. Some versions (for example, ESV) refer to 'treasures of darkness'.

We often glibly use Romans 8:28, 'In all things God works for the good of those who love him', to cover a multitude of life's tricky circumstances and irritations. But when we're going through that truly difficult valley, it can be hard to see the 'good', let alone any hidden treasure.

When I look back at the illness and limited ability of my younger life, they can seem like wasted years – years I might have been living a 'normal life', rather than gripped by agoraphobia, following what was eventually diagnosed as Ménière's disease.

Yet, now – by God's grace – I live that normal life. I look back and see how closely Jesus walked with me then. He was my constant companion. It set the foundation for the rest of my life. I found the riches that were stored in the secret place – although it wasn't a place I would have chosen to visit. The treasure, the riches, were found in being with God in times of solitude and worship, talking to and listening to him, being aware of his presence, when I could do little else.

I believe God uses times of darkness and of sometimes being 'set aside', in whatever context, to show us riches that we otherwise may not have noticed. Do you feel set aside? Look for the treasures of his company, of his love, of the reality of who he is. Our present and our future are with him. Called by our God, known by name, we are rich if we know him.

Are you going through a difficult time? As you ask God to reveal the 'hidden treasure' of his company and presence, be comforted. Don't be afraid. He is with you, and he'll never let you go.

SHEILA JACOBS

What God calls rich

'You say, "I am rich; I have acquired wealth and do not need a thing."
But you do not realise that you are wretched… poor… I counsel you to
buy from me gold refined in the fire, so that you can become rich.' (NIV)

It's so easy to start off with good intentions and finish up wondering where
it all went wrong! My family used to begin the day with a quiet time and
a praise CD in the car. Now we grab a quick breakfast and we're out the
door. We miss church and house group not because we are exhausted, but
because we're caught up with other things. The pressures of the world are
replacing our godly contentment (1 Timothy 6:6). Yes, we still pray, but we
don't spend quality time with God. Any relationship under those kinds of
conditions simply will not thrive.

What God calls 'rich' doesn't line up with the world's definition. It's
about growing relationship, discovering his company. It's about talking
and listening to him, worshipping him, reading his word and doing what
he says. It's about considering others who are on this journey called life
and being concerned about what will happen to them once their brief time
here is over. It's about sharing our lives and our resources. It's about being
generous, just as God is generous with us. It's about sowing into a heavenly
kingdom where we can lose nothing of our treasure whatever happens to
us in this life, because true riches don't belong to this earth.

Being rich towards God means building a whole life based in the one who
is life itself, far beyond the confines of the few years we have here and the
perishable things the world calls 'riches'. It's something we can never lose.

I hope these notes have encouraged you to review your heart – maybe
even your lifestyle. It can be difficult to make changes, but let's not strive
for the things we cannot keep, the things that will rot or rust away. Let our
focus be on something far greater – and eternal!

---

*Imagine Jesus knocking at your door. What would you like to say to him
about 'treasure' and about being rich towards him? What do you think he
might say to you?*

SHEILA JACOBS

Daniel

Rosemary Green writes:

Daniel is a book of two very different parts. The first six chapters appear straightforward, as they tell of the teenage Daniel and his friends being deported from Jerusalem, when Nebuchadnezzar, ruler of Babylon, invaded and conquered Judah, and staying true to their God against all opposition. There is much for us to learn, especially as we live in times when our country is becoming increasingly ignorant of Jesus, atheistic and antagonistic to a godly lifestyle.

The second half of the book describes the strange visions Daniel had of the future of the world. These visions are notoriously difficult to understand, so in the notes I have focused on the early chapters. But I have found John Lennox's book *Against the Flow* very helpful. He knows far more about Daniel than I ever will! If you want a good solid read to go deeper into Daniel, delve into this book.

There is some controversy about when the book of Daniel was written. Many liberal scholars say it is a collection of myths and could not have been written before the second century BC. I prefer to side with more conservative scholars who believe it was indeed written by Daniel in the sixth century BC. Nebuchadnezzar invaded Judah and the first Jews were deported in about 597BC, Daniel probably among them; Cyrus started to rule in 539BC. So Daniel was in Babylon for nearly 60 years, in a prominent position for much of that time (Daniel 1:21).

Babylon was a magnificent city, the largest in the world at the time. The roof gardens of the palace, the Hanging Gardens, were one of the seven wonders of the ancient world. There were over a thousand temples, as well as libraries and centres devoted to law, architecture and astronomy. It was a thriving university city as well as a commercial hub. Daniel and his friends must have been overawed when they arrived. But the message of the book is of a living God who is pre-eminent – the God of gods and Lord of lords, sovereign over all the gods and over the rulers of Babylon too. He is victorious and we can trust him.

Teenage faithfulness

Daniel resolved not to defile himself with the royal food and wine, and he asked the chief official for permission not to defile himself in this way. Now God had caused the official to show favour and compassion to Daniel, but the official told Daniel, 'I am afraid of my lord the king.' (NIV)

Three of my grandsons started at university recently. Leaving the cocoon of home comforts and school structures and learning new independence among peers intent on enjoying fresh freedom with alcohol and sex brought bigger challenges than they had expected. So we can imagine the shock for these deported teenagers, Daniel and his friends among them. They were well-born, of good physique and highly intelligent. But they were forcefully uprooted from everything familiar and transported to a new environment, with its strange culture and language and no prospect of a vacation at home after two months. They had no choice but to enrol in the Royal University of Babylon. They were even given new names, symbols of new identities that sought to expunge their Jewish heritage.

I guess that most of the deported students revelled in the lavishness of the royal diet and free-flowing wine – especially after the restrictions of living under siege in Jerusalem. But not Daniel. He had already behaved in a way that earned the respect of the chief official and the guard, so the path was cleared for him to ask for a short trial period of a vegetarian diet without alcohol. The chief official was scared of the king's 'off with his head' reaction if the youths appeared undernourished, but his underling was willing to try it. Does it look like a small request for Daniel to make? He was taking a huge risk in going against the stream in this alien environment.

The risk paid off. After ten days, the young men were healthier than their peers, and, with God's help, they excelled in their studies. First-class degrees for all of them! And Daniel in particular developed clear spiritual gifts.

One of my grandsons spelled out how difficult it can be to forego the extra drink and not to conform to student culture. In what ways do you find it hard to resist the prevailing norms and stand up for Christ's values and behaviour?
ROSEMARY GREEN

A young man's wisdom

Daniel returned to his house and explained the matter to his friends Hananiah, Mishael and Azariah. He urged them to plead for mercy from the God of heaven concerning this mystery, so that he and his friends might not be executed with the rest of the wise men of Babylon. (NIV)

King Nebuchadnezzar was unpredictable, to say the least! He wanted to know the meaning of his strange, frightening dream. But to ensure that no magician was inventing the interpretation, the king asked that they first told him the content of the dream. 'That's impossible!' they told him. 'Tell us what happened in your dream, and then we'll interpret it for you.' But the king was adamant. Tell him the dream and its meaning, and gifts and honour would be lavished on them. But no dream or interpretation? That would be rewarded by a grisly death.

They were perfectly rational in their corporate reply: 'What the king asks is too difficult. No one can reveal it to the king except the gods, and they do not live among humans' (v. 11). In one way they were right; but they didn't know the living God. Nebuchadnezzar, far from rational, lost his temper and ordered the execution of all his advisors.

The Jewish quartet heard of the king's edict only when guards came to arrest them. Daniel explored the situation with the colonel of the household cavalry, and then took another risk, going to the king to ask for a delay. Then, most importantly, he told his friends to pray. I'm sure they prayed fervently; execution was imminent!

I wish I were as ready as they were to turn to God with a need, for myself or for others – not only when the situation is as urgent as theirs was. I find it too easy to act first and pray afterwards. God in his graciousness gave Daniel a vision to show him the dream; Daniel's immediate response was to praise the almighty, sovereign God for his wisdom and for sharing that wisdom with his people, before he went back to the king with the interpretation.

In Acts 4, when the Jewish authorities ordered Peter and John to stop preaching about Jesus, they responded, 'We can't!' Their bold prayers in an impromptu prayer meeting with their friends were answered spectacularly.
ROSEMARY GREEN

Pause for praise

During the night the mystery was revealed to Daniel in a vision. Then Daniel praised the God of heaven and said, 'Praise be to the name of God forever and ever; wisdom and power are his.' (NIV)

Daniel and his friends had pleaded with God to reveal Nebuchadnezzar's dream; during the night he did exactly that. Daniel's immediate response was not just to thank God that he had answered their prayer, but also to stop and praise God for his character, before going back to the king with the interpretation.

I have often told the story of a small boy who broke his toy in a fit of temper. When Daddy returned home, the boy's 'prayers' to Dad included 'sorry for my temper', 'please mend it' and 'thank you' when it was done. And, as he watched the repair, he exclaimed, 'You're wonderful!', expressing his praise for who his dad was. That 'you're wonderful' is an aspect of prayer we often neglect. I wish I were as ready as Daniel was to praise the Lord for his character as well as to thank him for what he does for me.

Read through the song of praise again, and notice how Daniel praises God for his wisdom, for his authority over nature and over royalty and for the wisdom he gives to others, before thanking him specifically for the way he has answered prayer about the dream.

And now let's join in Daniel's praise to the Lord ourselves, based on these verses:

Praise be to your name, O God, forever and ever; wisdom and power are yours. You change times and seasons; you depose kings and raise up others. You give wisdom to the wise and knowledge to the discerning. You reveal deep and hidden things; you know what lies in darkness, and light dwells with you.

What other aspects of God's character do you want to include in your praise?

Lord, please help me to be more ready to thank you for what you do for me and to praise you more often for who you are.

ROSEMARY GREEN

God is my enabler

The king asked Daniel… 'Are you able to tell me what I saw in my dream and interpret it?' Daniel replied, 'No wise man, enchanter, magician or diviner can explain to the king the mystery he has asked about, but there is a God in heaven who reveals mysteries.' (NIV)

Throughout this chapter Daniel shows remarkable poise and peace. In one way he was walking on eggshells, with such a volatile king. But he was resting on his trust in the living God. He is a perfect example of Paul's words in Philippians 4:6–7: 'Do not be anxious about anything, but in every situation, by prayer and petition, with thanksgiving, present your requests to God. And the peace of God, which transcends all understanding, will guard your hearts and your minds in Christ Jesus.' He wasn't relying just on his vision in the night or on his friends' prayers; I believe he was listening to God step by step. He had no hesitation in affirming to the king that his wisdom came not from himself but from his God.

Are we as ready as he was to tell others about our God as the source of our abilities? He was then very clear in describing Nebuchadnezzar's dream and its interpretation.

As the king listened, he must have been pleased and flattered to hear that he was symbolised by the 'head of gold'. Then, as Daniel revealed more, the king was perhaps alarmed to hear of the future breakup of his kingdom. Yet Daniel's bearing conveyed so clearly the reality of his God that Nebuchadnezzar not only kept the promise we read yesterday of power, honour and lavish gifts for the one who could tell him all about his dream, he also acknowledged that Daniel's God was indeed 'the God of gods and the Lord of kings'.

That is the sort of impact we want to have on those we meet: we may not be interpreting their dreams, but we can be reflecting the nature of Jesus.

Lord, may I have a listening ear and the same confidence to witness to your power in my life.

ROSEMARY GREEN

Stick your neck out

'If we are thrown into the blazing furnace, the God we serve is able to deliver us from it… But even if he does not, we want you to know, Your Majesty, that we will not serve your gods or worship the image of gold you have set up.' (NIV)

Have you ever had the disappointment of thinking a friend has made a profession of faith but then hasn't stuck to it? When Daniel had described and interpreted the king's dream, Nebuchadnezzar acknowledged that Daniel's God was indeed 'the God of gods and the Lord of kings'. Sadly, that admission was short-lived. Perhaps Daniel's words, 'You are that head of gold', had gone to his head. Certainly his pride took over; he didn't want anyone else to be lord over him. Nebuchadnezzar ensured that everyone knew the extent of his power. His golden statue, 30 metres tall and four metres wide, could not be ignored, and the penalty for disobeying the command to fall down and worship it would be death in the fiery furnace.

Thanks to Daniel's listening to the Lord, the king's threat to kill all the magicians and astrologers who failed to explain his dream had not been put into practice. But the ungrateful advisors saw Daniel and his friends elevated to important positions and were jealous of these young foreign upstarts. They said, 'Your Majesty, those Jews are ignoring your edict to worship the golden image.'

True to form, the irate king summoned the rebels. Although faced with almost certain death, they were resolute. They trusted a God who could do a miracle and rescue them. And if he didn't? No way would they serve the Babylonian gods or worship Nebuchadnezzar's statue. They knew the ten commandments and were determined to obey. No idol worship for them. They would not retract and were outspoken in their convictions. What an example they set us!

What are the more subtle temptations we face to be less bold in our witness to Jesus?

ROSEMARY GREEN

Bound but free

'Praise be to the God of Shadrach, Meshach and Abednego, who has sent his angel and rescued his servants! They trusted in him and defied the king's command and were willing to give up their lives rather than serve or worship any god except their own God.' (NIV)

The enraged king did his utmost to ensure that the three bound Jews would perish painfully and speedily. But the tables turned dramatically. The flames were so fierce that even the soldiers throwing them into the furnace were burned alive. But the three prisoners were unharmed. Even Nebuchadnezzar saw an angel walking with them in the furnace, unbound as they now were. He called to them to come out – a command they obeyed, unlike his previous orders. They walked out free, totally untouched by the fire. Their confidence in God, whom they had declared could rescue them, was vindicated.

And the king changed his tune. He acknowledged their faith in God and their courage in disobeying him. More importantly, he recognised God's power. While he stopped short of decreeing that all should worship the Jewish God, he made it an offence for anyone to say anything against that God.

Nebuchadnezzar saw a miracle, and his attitude changed. But it does not always happen. However clearly, however powerfully God is at work, the sceptical may ignore the evidence. Do you remember Jesus' grief over Chorazin and Bethsaida? 'Woe to you, Chorazin! Woe to you, Bethsaida! For if the miracles that were performed in you had been performed in Tyre and Sidon, they would have repented long ago in sackcloth and ashes,' Jesus said in distress (Matthew 11:21). The people in those towns had seen miracles, yet they continued to ignore Jesus. It is the same today. I think of a young woman in our church who was the talk of the hospital after she was miraculously, astonishingly healed – but her unbelieving parents remained sceptical. We cannot count on evident miracles, powerful preaching or consistent witness to persuade people to believe, if they are not willing to change their minds, wills and lives.

Lord, I pray that you may give, and I may take, opportunities to act and speak for you. But I know that people need your Spirit to help them believe and change. Please show me the individuals you want me to pray for particularly.
ROSEMARY GREEN

Pride precedes a fall

I, Nebuchadnezzar, was at home in my palace, contented and prosperous. I had a dream that made me afraid. As I was lying in bed, the images and visions that passed through my mind terrified me. (NIV)

Nebuchadnezzar was a man with considerable spiritual awareness, and he was sure that this new dream about the huge tree had some special message. He consulted his large retinue of supposed wise men, but none could help. Finally he turned to Daniel, relying on Daniel's spiritual powers to explain what the vivid dream meant. But even though he had acknowledged earlier that Daniel's God gave his servant special insight, he was not yet ready to submit to that God.

In theory, he was. He declared, 'The decision is announced by messengers, the holy ones declare the verdict, so that the living may know that the Most High is sovereign over all kingdoms on earth and gives them to anyone he wishes and sets over them the lowliest of people' (v. 17). He said, 'The Most High is sovereign', but Nebuchadnezzar was still too keen on his own importance! Was he, perhaps, a little afraid that the dream might be telling him about his own downfall? I doubt it. He was too sure of himself – as he said, 'contented and prosperous'. He was king over a mighty empire; he thought he was supreme, untouchable.

Before we come down too hard on Nebuchadnezzar, let's look closer to home. We can all use words that declare right beliefs, yet don't allow those truths to affect our 'heart belief' or our lifestyle. For many years I recited the creed and I didn't doubt that Jesus was divine. But I failed to see how that connected with me. I needed to grasp my own sin and my need for Christ's Spirit in my life for Jesus to become alive and relevant. Even as a Christian of many years' standing, I can go through the motions of faith without really allowing my beliefs to penetrate my heart, my will, my relationship with God or my lifestyle.

Lord, I don't want to be a hypocrite. I want my attitudes and my behaviour to match my words.

ROSEMARY GREEN

The difficulty of confrontation

'This is the decree the Most High has issued against my lord the king… Your Majesty, be pleased to accept my advice: renounce your sins by doing what is right, and your wickedness by being kind to the oppressed. It may be that then your prosperity will continue.' (NIV)

Poor Daniel! He was in a difficult position. How was he to explain to the king what the dream meant without giving offence? He was terrified and hesitated to tell Nebuchadnezzar what God had shown him. The king saw his alarm and, surprisingly, encouraged him to go ahead. We are often afraid to confront someone with an uncomfortable truth, especially when that person is our superior. If God tells us to speak, we need to obey – but make sure it is God prompting us, not just our own feelings.

I notice Daniel's wisdom and tact. He warned him subtly that it was not all good news, but then spoke positively – 'Your Majesty, you are that tree! You have become great and strong' (v. 22) – before he moved on to the bad news. The tree would be cut down. Nebuchadnezzar would not only lose his position, but he would also be mad for a time, as he lived and ate with wild animals in disarray, before he was restored to sanity and to his kingdom. Daniel was forthright: 'Renounce your sins and wickedness. Repent. Change your ways.' The king didn't lose his temper, as Daniel might have feared. But, sadly, neither did he pay attention – well, not enough to make changes, as verses 29–30 make clear.

It is never easy to rebuke in a way that avoids causing offence and will be listened to. However faithful we are, our hearers can choose whether or not they pay attention. I remember telling my elderly mother in no uncertain terms that she was wrong when she was ranting against a daughter-in-law's well-intended but misplaced act of kindness. To my relief, she accepted the rebuke meekly (though what she said later to the offender, I never learnt).

Lord, I pray that when I need to rebuke anyone that I can be gentle, truthful, faithful and effective.

ROSEMARY GREEN

God's word is true

A voice came from heaven, 'This is what is decreed for you, King Nebuchadnezzar: your royal authority has been taken from you. You will be driven away from people… until you acknowledge that the Most High is sovereign over all kingdoms on earth and gives them to anyone he wishes.' (NIV)

We often complain that things don't happen as fast as we expect! Daniel may have wondered why there was a year's delay before anything dramatic happened. Peter tells us, 'The Lord is not slow in keeping his promise… Instead he is patient with you, not wanting anyone to perish, but everyone to come to repentance' (2 Peter 3:9). God in his graciousness gave the king ample time to change. But Nebuchadnezzar was as full of himself as ever. He strutted on the roof surveying the scene, saying, 'Is not this the great Babylon I have built as the royal residence, by my mighty power and for the glory of my majesty?' (v. 30).

Then God acted, suddenly. Secular history tells us nothing about Nebuchadnezzar's seven years of madness, but it was clearly a severe breakdown of his mental health. He must have been a sorry sight. Yet he did not lose all reason, and one day he came to his senses. He came to acknowledge God as supreme sovereign over the world.

As I read these last verses, I sense that this time his submission to God was real and wholehearted. 'Now I, Nebuchadnezzar, praise and exalt and glorify the King of heaven, because everything he does is right and all his ways are just. And those who walk in pride he is able to humble' (v. 37). That was a testimony to his own experience.

'Everything he does is right.' Do you believe that? I love Moses' affirmation: 'He is the Rock, his works are perfect, and all his ways are just. A faithful God who does no wrong, upright and just is he' (Deuteronomy 32:4). I have come to see that there would be no point in trusting a god who was wrong even 1% of the time.

Meditate on verses 34–35 and on Deuteronomy 32:4. Ask yourself how far you believe in God's absolute supremacy and in his total rightness – even when you cannot understand why he is allowing apparent tragedies to happen.

ROSEMARY GREEN

The perils of sacrilege

'You had the goblets from his temple brought to you, and you... drank wine from them. You praised the gods of silver and gold... which cannot see or hear or understand. But you did not honour the God who holds in his hand your life and all your ways.' (NIV)

Belshazzar was even more arrogant than Nebuchadnezzar (his ancestor, not actually his father). When Nebuchadnezzar conquered Jerusalem, he carried from the temple the vessels dedicated for worship and stored them in the museum in Babylon. Daniel must have hated that – the precious vessels dedicated to his God. But at least Nebuchadnezzar didn't use them. Belshazzar had no such compunction.

A huge banquet, for the nobles and all their women, became his excuse to use the golden goblets from Jerusalem. It was the biggest mistake of his life. As they used the Lord's cups to drink their toasts to the dead gods of Babylon, they saw human fingers writing on the wall. Terrified, Belshazzar summoned all the country's astrologers, but none could understand it. The queen appeared and reminded him about Daniel, the man on whom his predecessor had relied for spiritual interpretations.

So Daniel was called. He was not interested in Belshazzar's offers of gifts or honour, but he was willing to speak plainly: remember your ancestor. When Nebuchadnezzar was powerful and proud, he was stripped of his glory and became insane until he humbled himself before God. You knew all this, Daniel said to Belshazzar, but took no notice, so the words on the wall speak of God's judgement, of the end of your reign, of your inadequacies and of the fact that your kingdom will be split between the Medes and the Persians. Belshazzar's death was immediate, and the kingdom passed to the Medes.

We may ask why there was such sudden judgement on Belshazzar compared with the delay for Nebuchadnezzar. While we are not given more detail, the impression we are left with is of a man who was steeped in pride and sin, and whose misuse of the holy vessels was his final act of defiance against God.

We can readily condemn Belshazzar's blatant disregard of God's ways: 'No other gods before me. No idols. Keep my name holy.' I suggest we reread the ten commandments and ask ourselves how careful we are to obey them.

ROSEMARY GREEN

To pray or not to pray

When Daniel learned that the decree had been published, he went home to his upstairs room where the windows opened towards Jerusalem. Three times a day he got down on his knees and prayed, giving thanks to his God, just as he had done before. (NIV)

Jealousy is a nasty trait. The green-eyed monster often rears its ugly head when we least expect it. Jealousy of another's money, relationships, popularity, position… any one can creep in. The antidote? 'Be content with what you have, because God has said, "Never will I leave you; never will I forsake you"' (Hebrews 13:5). The author to the Hebrews was writing about money, but we can apply their remedy to any jealous temptation. Be content with Christ himself and with what he gives us.

The new king Darius had noticed Daniel's exceptional abilities and planned to make him top dog in his administration. Civil servants had probably hoped that the new ruler would bypass Daniel. This interloping exile from Judah! They could find no basis for charges against Daniel, given his gifts and integrity; instead, they saw his faith as his soft underbelly. So they agreed to appeal to Darius' pride: 'Your Majesty, why not issue an edict that anyone who prays to any god or human besides yourself in the next month shall be thrown into the lions' den? Write it down; the laws of the Medes and Persians cannot be revoked!'

Was this a problem for Daniel? Apparently not. His habit was to go to his room three times daily to pray – not secretly, but openly. He puts me to shame. I have my set time daily to read my Bible and to pray, but I often waste it. Only God sees my failure – but that is no excuse. Daniel knew his jealous enemies, and the edict, but nothing would stop him praying.

The king was trapped! Daniel's enemies had reminded him of the unchangeable decree before they told him of Daniel's disobedience. No way could he lose face and retract the order. All he could do was to declare his faith in Daniel's God.

Lord, I don't need all Daniel's abilities. Please help me to be content with what you have given me. But I do want to share his commitment to prayer. I confess I often fail. Please help me, each day.

ROSEMARY GREEN

The tables turned

Daniel answered, 'May the king live forever! My God sent his angel, and he shut the mouths of the lions. They have not hurt me, because I was found innocent in his sight. Nor have I ever done any wrong before you, Your Majesty.' (NIV)

Secular sources tell us that Darius' main belief was in the god Asha, but he supported the religions of other parts of his empire. His faith in Daniel's God is remarkable, as he recognised Daniel's abilities and his commitment to his God. Poor Darius! He didn't want Daniel thrown to the lions. But he was paying the price for succumbing to his administrators' flattery.

There seemed no way out. The entrance to the den was sealed, with Daniel inside, and Darius spent a long, sleepless night. At the crack of dawn he was out of his bed and out to the den. How he hoped for an answer (not the roar of well-fed lions) to his despairing call to Daniel! Daniel's reply was confident. He had no doubt that God had protected him; no doubt, either, of his own innocence before God and the king. Darius expected him to need help out of the den, but Daniel was totally unharmed. And the sequel, Daniel's enemies denounced and destroyed, shows that the lions were indeed hungry!

Just because Daniel was protected by God in this miraculous way does not mean that God's followers always escape from painful death. Many Christian martyrs have died at the hands of evil men. I am privileged to have known Archbishop Janani Luwum, murdered in Uganda for his denunciation of President Idi Amin. But I am convinced, with the apostle Paul, that 'neither death nor life, neither angels nor demons, neither the present nor the future, nor any powers, neither height nor depth, nor anything else in all creation, will be able to separate us from the love of God that is in Christ Jesus our Lord' (Romans 8:38–39). We are utterly safe in God's hands – safe for eternal life, not always for life on earth.

Let's learn Romans 8:38–39 by heart (with its Bible reference). And if you know those verses already, then learn Darius' affirmation of God in Daniel 6:26–27.
ROSEMARY GREEN

We have sinned

Lord, the great and awesome God, who keeps his covenant of love with those who love him and keep his commandments, we have sinned and done wrong. We have been wicked and have rebelled; we have turned away from your commands and laws. (NIV)

Jeremiah made it clear that the deportation to Babylon was God's judgement on a persistently disobedient people (Jeremiah 25:8–11). He prophesied that the exile would last 70 years, and though there are doubts about who Darius was and when he ruled, this prayer was towards the end of those 70 years. Daniel, now an old man, reflected on the sin of kings and people that had brought them there.

I see depth and straightforwardness in his confession. He acknowledged that God is a great God, who was faithful in his love towards his people, who brought them out of slavery in Egypt, and who was merciful and forgiving. In contrast he saw a people who were rebellious and determinedly disobedient. So 'all this disaster has come on us, yet we have not sought the favour of the Lord our God by turning from our sins and giving attention to your truth' (v. 13). Repentance was needed.

Daniel had a deep sense of shame, and I wonder if nowadays we emphasise God's love but ignore him as judge and treat our sin too lightly. I have just reread the confession we used to say regularly in church, from the old Anglican prayer book: 'Almighty God, Father of our Lord Jesus Christ and maker of all things, judge of all men: we acknowledge and bewail our manifold sins and wickedness, which we, from time to time, most grievously have committed, by thought, word and deed, against thy divine Majesty, provoking most justly thy wrath and indignation against us. We do earnestly repent and are heartily sorry for these our misdoings; the remembrance of them is grievous unto us; the burden of them is intolerable.' Heavy words, that express deep grief for sin – sin that really matters in the eyes of a holy God.

Awareness of sin needn't leave us in despair; it can lead us to joyful appreciation of God's love and forgiveness. As Daniel prayed, 'We do not make requests of you because we are righteous, but because of your great mercy' (v. 18).

ROSEMARY GREEN

A stupendous vision

I looked, and there before me was one like a son of man, coming with the clouds of heaven. He approached the Ancient of Days and was led into his presence. He was given authority, glory and sovereign power; all nations and peoples of every language worshipped him. (NIV)

Daniel must have been amazed as he watched the vision unfolding before him. First, there were four strange beasts, the fourth one terrifyingly destructive, with a small boastful horn. Then our reading picks up as, in his vision, he saw the 'Ancient of Days', the Father God, seated on a throne, surrounded by millions of angels. The judgement began, and the fourth beast was killed.

The vision proceeded, with the son of man coming with the clouds of heaven. Jesus himself used this image as he told his disciples of his return, not in the human form they knew him, but in glory and power as king (Matthew 24:30–31). Many have tried to interpret the beasts as different empires, either in Daniel's era or later in history. I am more concerned that we see the main threads. However evil the beasts, whatever persecution and suffering may come, we can have no doubt that the living God is the ultimate victor and that his Son will come in glory, as judge, to reign eternally: 'His dominion is an everlasting dominion that will not pass away, and his kingdom is one that will never be destroyed' (v. 14).

The first six chapters of the book of Daniel showed us Daniel and his friends subject to different challenges. Each time they stood up for the living God, determined to obey him whatever the cost. The trio knew they might not emerge from the fiery furnace, though in fact in each story we see the saints triumphant and the proud god-ignoring rulers humbled. These incidents point towards the eternal fulfilment of God's purposes, with Father and Son reigning and evil destroyed. That is the confidence we can have, as we set our gaze beyond life on earth to life in eternity.

Join with the angels' praise in John's similar vision six centuries later, in Revelation 4—5. Father, please help me to look beyond life on earth, and give me a glimpse of your glory and your eternal reign.

ROSEMARY GREEN

Hope for no-hopers

Jennifer Rees Larcombe writes:

Most of us, during a lifetime, face at least one apparently hopeless situation. There seems no obvious way out of it and the resulting helplessness causes us to start making endless plans for escape. Our ideas go round and round in our heads as we ask for help from everyone we know and consult experts, while their conflicting advice confuses us still further. If we have faith, we pray more urgently than ever before.

Years ago I heard a sermon entitled 'Shut up to a miracle' by Revd Alan Redpath, who recounted how Moses had finally managed to escape from Pharaoh along with several million slaves, plus their children and livestock, only to discover their way was blocked by the sea in front, steep cliffs on either side and Egypt's army in hot pursuit behind them. Everyone started blaming Moses for their hopeless predicament (people always want someone to blame), but Moses merely said, 'Stand firm… The Lord will fight for you; you need only to be still' (Exodus 14:13–14, NIV).

Naturally we pray when life is collapsing around us, but so often when nothing seems to change, we step up our heavenly bombardment with endless prayers which often don't seem to work. This is because prayer must be partnered by trust in God's ability and desire to help. Without the willingness to wait for him to act at the time he knows is best, our endless nagging prayers can simply become another form of worry.

During my worst ever 'no-hope situation', I didn't realise that faith which is willing to wait doesn't come naturally. We have to specifically *ask* for it! So I was soon sucked down into a spiral of question marks – 'Why has God let all this happen to me? Isn't he as powerful as I thought, or perhaps he just doesn't love me?'

My faith was being smothered by doubts. One day as I sat watching a programme about koalas, I saw the mothers leaping fearlessly through tall trees with their babies desperately clinging to their fur. I suddenly realised that I needed to stop asking questions and trying to solve my problems, and instead cling to God as trustingly as a baby koala clings to its mother. It sounds simplistic, but oh how it helped! When we are 'shut up to a miracle', we just have to be still and let God be God (Psalm 46:10).

Who's to blame?

Sarai said to Abram, 'This is all your fault!...' Abram replied, 'Look, she is your servant, so deal with her as you see fit.' Then Sarai treated Hagar so harshly that she finally ran away. (NLT)

Who do you think Hagar blamed for her hopeless situation? Herself, for running away? Sarai, for using and abusing a helpless foreign girl in her power? Or Abram? Abram failed by not asking God's guidance before sleeping with a slave and then refusing to become involved in the consequences.

Anyone who has endured years of yearning for a baby will relate to Sarai's all-consuming pain. Perhaps the 'surrogate mother' idea appealed because she would at least have Abram's baby to care for and love. Did she simply snap when Hagar proudly reminded her that, as mother of the heir, she would be the chief wife, respected by the entire tribe?

We waste so much time looking for someone to blame for our predicaments instead of asking God for help. Hagar would not have dared to speak to God; in her society a female runaway slave was worthless. She was in great danger, facing nothing but more abuse or death.

Many women, for a number of reasons, live with a sense of worthlessness or of being not quite good enough. Loneliness is widespread too, even inside marriage, when we feel we don't really matter to anyone. If you've ever felt like that, you'll realise how Hagar was feeling when God spoke directly to her. Slaves were never noticed or spoken to, unless to be given orders. But here was God himself talking directly to her! 'The angel of the Lord' implies that God himself spoke.

He wanted her (and us) to know that he cared about all she had gone through, that she was important to him for who she was, as well as who he could help her become.

Lord, I often feel so useless and insignificant. Help me remember that there is no one in all the world more important to you than I am.

JENNIFER REES LARCOMBE

Worst fear

**So Jacob was left alone, and a man wrestled with him till daybreak…
Jacob replied, 'I will not let you go unless you bless me.'… So Jacob
called the place Peniel, saying, 'It is because I saw God face to face.'
(NIV)**

If you have a temperament like mine, you frequently experience your worst-
case scenarios via your imagination, and when these scenarios actually play
out, they are usually better than expected!

Jacob was probably always scared of his macho brother Esau, who felt
no need for God, while Jacob longed for God's favour and the blessing
promised to his grandfather Abraham. When he finally stole that blessing from Esau (Genesis 27:3–28), he had to flee abroad from his brother's
murderous rage. He stayed away for many years, marrying two wives and
becoming vastly wealthy – but he never lost that terrible dread.

Do you have a worst fear? It might be cancer, dementia or the loss of your
parent, partner or child. One day God asked Jacob to face his fear by meeting Esau again (Genesis 31:13). Instead of praying and trusting the promises
God had already given him (Genesis 28:15), Jacob began endlessly planning
ways to defend himself and his possessions. He even tried to pacify Esau
with promises of lavish gifts, only to discover Esau was advancing with an
army. Finally, Jacob prayed, but rather than waiting for God's protection,
he dashed off again making elaborate plans. Then suddenly, in the middle
of his worst nightmares, he encountered God.

The same thing happened to me once. For years I dreaded a particular
situation, but when it happened it brought me closer to God than ever
before and became my greatest blessing. When we realise we have actually
survived the worst, fear is conquered.

If we are prone to anxiety, it can either make us more dependent on
God, as we frequently turn to him for help, or drive us from him, because
we feel that, in order to be safe, we ourselves must take control of everyone
and everything.

---

*Lord, when it is desperately difficult to trust you, give me the kind of
determination to hold on to you that Jacob had.*

JENNIFER REES LARCOMBE

Power of the mind

Joseph's master took him and put him in prison… But while Joseph was there in the prison, the Lord was with him; he showed him kindness and granted him favour in the eyes of the prison warder. (NIV)

In Joseph's place, would our account read like this? – 'The door slammed shut, plunging the dungeon into darkness. Surely this is the end, I thought, I'll never get out of here! Surely the God my father worshipped can't abandon me like this. I thought he had when my jealous brothers sold me into slavery, but I worked so hard that I rose to managing a whole household. I believed God had helped me then, but if he's going to let me be kicked back into worse hopelessness, I'm giving up trying to please him.'

Most of us might have thought like that. Obviously, Joseph did not or he would never have behaved so well in that terrible place, which eventually led him into fame and fortune and enabled him to save his family and nation from extinction.

Hopeless situations are only hopeless if we think they are. It is what we think about them that determines how we feel, react and behave. When we start to think that God has totally failed us and question his power and love, we soon begin to feel bitter, abandoned and afraid.

The apostle Paul was also unjustly flung into prison after being badly beaten, but he refused to think negatively and sang God's praises at the top of his voice. In other words, he started to rejoice by willpower and then discovered he *felt* full of joy (Acts 16:23–27). He told us to rejoice, whatever the circumstances (Philippians 4:4). I wish I could say I did that during my bad times, but it usually takes me a while to realise it's impossible to change my thinking during a trauma, unless I ask for God's help – which is tricky, but vital, when I'm mad with him!

The key to Joseph's success in prison is found in verse 21. However horrible it was, he held on to the fact that God was present with him and God was kind.

JENNIFER REES LARCOMBE

Lost love

Now Moses was tending the flock of Jethro his father-in-law, the priest of Midian, and he led the flock to the far side of the wilderness and came to Horeb, the mountain of God. There the angel of the Lord appeared to him. (NIV)

Not all hopeless situations are caused by dramatic events. Some creep up on us so gradually that we don't even realise we are stuck in one. Even though Moses had been adopted by an Egyptian princess, he grew up knowing he had been born a Hebrew and that his destiny was to free his oppressed people. His birth mother, hired as his nurse, would have helped him realise that.

As a young prince, this ambition had burned so brightly that he tried to achieve it in his own strength and had to escape Egypt labelled a murderer. That was 40 years earlier, and since then nothing significant had happened. He had married, settled down and, perhaps because he had totally lost his confidence, taken what was considered the least important job of all, shepherding. He didn't even own his own sheep.

When God suddenly spoke and told him to go and do the job he had once longed to do, he felt it was now impossible. Hopelessness had crippled him; he might have died a few years later, never having become one of the greatest figures in history.

Sometimes I wonder how many potential Moses-like people there have been. When they were new Christians, they burned with enthusiasm for God, seeing themselves doing something amazing for his kingdom. Then, after a few setbacks, they became content to be nominal Christians, with God confined to a small part of their lives.

Could it have been like that for you? Have pressures, disappointments or even good things pushed God out of the middle of your life? What experiences could be like Moses' experience of suddenly meeting with God at that burning bush? Perhaps you are even now arguing with God because the cost may feel too great?

Lord, I sometimes feel I'm in a lethargic wilderness, aimlessly walking in circles. Perhaps I'm scared of doing anything new for you. If you should call me, help me to be ready.

JENNIFER REES LARCOMBE

Not enough faith?

Gideon replied, 'But how can I save Israel? My clan is the weakest in Manasseh, and I am the least in my family.' The Lord answered, 'I will be with you.' (NIV)

When my fourth baby became seriously ill, our whole church joined us in prayer, but to me, the situation seemed hopeless; I was convinced my baby was not getting better because of my lack of faith. When I confessed this to our vicar, he simply said, 'Stop trying to work up your faith; relax and ask a faithful God to grow faith inside you.'

At the beginning of Gideon's story, he obviously has no faith; he's timid, resentful and lacks self-confidence, and he only has a vague belief in God – definitely not the kind of leader his nation needed in their desperate situation. In any job interview, Gideon would have been written off as hopeless, but things always change after we meet God himself. Gideon's mysterious encounter was not with a mere angel. When we read 'angel of the Lord' in the Old Testament, it means God himself, appearing as a being long before Jesus came. Notice what God called Gideon. A 'mighty warrior' was the last thing Gideon was, and he knew it. God knew it too, but went on to point out that when Gideon had God with him, he would have all the resources of heaven at his disposal. It took Gideon a lot more convincing before he finally realised he had actually met God himself and even more before he realised that God is always bigger than the problems we face. Sometimes our faith fails to grow because our vision of God is far smaller than he actually is.

Can you remember a time when you encountered God? What difference did that make to you?

In spite of Gideon's endless demands for reassurance, he did go on to lead his nation to victory.

A remarkable lady who founded a huge Christian organisation once told me, 'The only qualification we need for ministry is to know our own inadequacy and trust in God's perfect adequacy.'

JENNIFER REES LARCOMBE

Extraordinary generosity

'First make a small loaf of bread for me… then make something for yourself and your son. For this is what the Lord, the God of Israel, says: "The jar of flour will not be used up and the jug of oil will not run dry until the day the Lord sends rain on the land."' (NIV)

Yet again the people of Israel were forsaking God to worship Baal, whom they believed controlled the weather. So God's message, through Elijah, was a direct challenge to Baal. Neither dew nor rain would fall for years unless God willed it.

Once the awful consequences of drought became obvious, Elijah only survived because of God's provision, and once his secret water supply vanished, he was forced to escape abroad.

Now comes the fascinating mystery behind this story. The young widow would have been brought up to worship Baal – no one in her country knew about Yahweh, so how did she? I'll ask her when we meet in heaven! She not only knew about him but heard his voice and respected him enough to obey what he asked her to do. She had no Bible, church, prayer support or fellowship, all the things we Christians today take for granted. Yet her faith was enormous – no wonder Jesus himself remembered her with pride (Luke 4:25–26). He also noticed another widow, who gave to God her last coins rather than buy herself food. He always notices and appreciates the kind little things we do in secret.

People in hopeless situations usually focus on self-preservation, feeling that they must 'look after number one'. This widow would have sold all she had to buy enough for one last meal, before watching her child die. Could you give away your family's last meal? Her faith and generosity astound me!

God loves generosity, perhaps because he is so generous himself, so we can never out-give him. Not only did they all three eat well throughout the drought, but the little boy was also restored to life.

Someone once told me, 'When things are so terrible that you can't get help, you can always give it.'

JENNIFER REES LARCOMBE

Burnout

Elijah was afraid and fled for his life… He sat down under a solitary broom tree and prayed that he might die. 'I have had enough, Lord,' he said. (NLT)

Perhaps the worst kinds of hopeless situations are not actually hopeless – we only think they are. Exhaustion and burnout caused Elijah's depression. Because he longed to see the nation turning back to God, he had spent months gathering them together to demonstrate the bogus claims of Baal worshippers and the power and reality of Yahweh. It had been a magnificent success, but when the opposition got too much for him, Elijah was too tired to think straight, so he bolted, feeling an utter failure and the only one in Israel who still believed in God – when actually there were 7,000 other believers.

Depression, like a grey cloud, can smother our perception of truth. The situation was far from hopeless: God was about to use Elijah to facilitate a glorious spiritual awakening.

I love the way God gave Elijah time to recover. He did not stand over him saying, 'Pull yourself together! Where's your faith?', as some Christians might. Instead God refreshed his mind with rest and sleep and nourished his body with good food; then he took him away alone to refresh his spirit.

Being alone with God is far more restorative than many of us realise. When my six children were small, spending daily time with God was hard. My friend Penny had four kids and felt the same. So, each term we gave each other a day to be with God at a local retreat house, while the other had all ten kids. Those days were so precious!

When Elijah reached Mount Sinai, where God first gave the commandments which his people were now ignoring, Elijah was reluctant to meet God; all he could do was pour out his negative thoughts. But still God waited patiently until Elijah was ready to hear his plans for the future.

Have you ever been smothered by depression – perhaps after a bereavement, major loss, accident or illness? I have. Seeing how God gave Elijah time to mend helped me greatly, and so did reminding myself, 'This will pass.'

JENNIFER REES LARCOMBE

Is he enough?

Her husband Elkanah would say to her, 'Hannah, why are you weeping? Why don't you eat? Why are you downhearted? Don't I mean more to you than ten sons?' (NIV)

Perhaps those annual visits to Shiloh to worship felt like repetitive 'hopeless situations' to Hannah – and her spiteful rival knew it. When you are badly hurt, do you find it hard to pour out your pain to God? For a woman back then, childlessness was seen as shameful, a punishment for sin, cutting her off from God. So Hannah's desperation must have lent her courage. Sadly, we often miss God's comfort because of shame from our past. Have your regrets and 'if onlys' ever made you feel uncomfortable about spending time with God?

As a single person, one Sunday morning in church I remember feeling miserable because of the way an older couple in the row in front of me frequently held hands. The sermon was based on Elkanah's question in verse 8, and I felt God was asking me, 'Am I not enough?'

Was my desire for a husband actually more important to me than God himself? I needed to think deeply about that.

On his 50th birthday, I remember a friend saying, 'After 50, it's loss after loss all the way.' Nowadays I'm realising how right he was. Unless we are very fortunate, we gradually lose people and activities that we always relied on for security and happiness. Surely it is vital to try to make the Lord himself our 'nearest and dearest', and to make our foremost goal to know him and please him. I'm still working on that – but after 25 years I have to say God has been a wonderful husband to me!

Lord, I lay out before you the desires of my heart. Change them if they are not your will for me, or give me the perseverance to go on praying.

JENNIFER REES LARCOMBE

Disillusionment

My God, my God, why have you forsaken me? Why are you so far from saving me, so far from my cries of anguish? (NIV)

The first hopeless situation David experienced only looked hopeless to his eyewitnesses. The onlookers saw an adolescent boy, without armour or sword, approaching a gigantic, seasoned warrior – obviously the boy would lose. David knew he would win, because he trusted in the power of God (see 1 Samuel 17:45–46), who had already told him he would live to be the next king (1 Samuel 16:1–13). After killing Goliath, David was made commander-in-chief of the army, married the king's daughter and was loved and admired by the whole nation. King Saul doted on him and David in return honoured and admired him. When everything suddenly changed, David found himself hiding in the wilderness, an outlaw, disillusioned by the king he had admired.

Have you ever looked up to a Christian leader, wanted to be like them, to follow in their footsteps, and then been bitterly disillusioned by them? Or maybe your disillusionment came from disappointment with God? Did you feel he had let you down, misled you completely?

Disappointment hurts badly and can cause us to feel separated from God, but we always have a choice: either we close our hearts against the Lord or we keep pressing into him by willpower.

It is obvious that David chose the second option. Today's psalm, probably written during his wilderness experience, clearly shows us how he tackled his dilemma. He reminded himself who God was, recalled God's track record, told God honestly how he felt, kept on crying out for God's help and began telling others about God's faithfulness. Soon other 'no-hopers' were joining David. Out in that bleak desert, he rebuilt their faith and confidence by turning them into a well-trained army (1 Samuel 22:2). God really can use our worst experiences to bring us good.

Lord, please help me to forgive any Christian leaders who have disillusioned me. Never let me put another human being on such a high pedestal that I worship them instead of you.

JENNIFER REES LARCOMBE

Angry neighbours

After this, Jesus went out and saw a tax collector by the name of Levi sitting at his tax booth. 'Follow me,' Jesus said to him, and Levi got up, left everything and followed him. (NIV)

According to his religious neighbours, Levi, later called Matthew, was a hopeless case. There would be no hope of God's mercy for a greedy predator like him. Most of the town loathed him, because collaborators grew rich by pocketing a share of the cruel tax levied by Rome. It was a lonely place to be, but I wonder how Matthew had fallen that low.

It is obvious from his gospel that he was highly educated, steeped in Jewish history and the Old Testament – fascinated by all the ancient prophesies which he later realised had been fulfilled in Jesus. Perhaps, as a boy, he had studied hard, longing to be chosen by one of the great theology schools in the temple, which led to a career as a venerated rabbi. Something had gone wrong which left him feeling a rejected failure.

He must have wondered what the point of all those years of study had been. Now he was nothing but a despised taxman, stuck in a shabby booth near the quayside – nothing but a parasite on his own people, seen by them as scum.

Perhaps he had heard Jesus preaching on the nearby beach, felt disgusted at what he had become and longed to start all over again, but thought that it was all too late now. Then that shadow had fallen over his accounts book, and one look into the face of Jesus restored his lost hope. Without a second thought, Matthew left the day's takings and followed.

It caused outrage in the community when Jesus not only went to supper with Matthew and his collaborating friends but also then chose him as one of his disciples. People have always found it hard to believe how completely Jesus can change someone!

Thank you, Lord, that with you it is never too late to change. You can also use all our experiences to shape us, even those we thought were a waste of time.
JENNIFER REES LARCOMBE

Who are you – really?

Jesus looked at him and loved him. 'One thing you lack,' he said. 'Go, sell everything you have and give to the poor, and you will have treasure in heaven. Then come, follow me.' (NIV)

Who do you think felt hopeless in this story? Certainly not the wealthy young man. As the complete opposite to Matthew, he would have been respected by everyone in his community for his godly lifestyle and good works.

Yet, in spite of everything he had going for him, there was obviously something about Jesus that fascinated him. He knelt, as he would to any venerated teacher; but was calling Jesus 'good' simply a flattering greeting? I wonder if Jesus' reply was a challenge, 'Do you just think of me as a good teacher, or are you wondering if I am the Messiah?' That is the challenge the world has faced ever since – if Jesus is God, then we must follow and obey him. It is easier for most people to think he was merely a good man.

The ruler's question could just have been a test to see if Jesus agreed with his belief that keeping all the commandments would take him safely to heaven.

I believe it was Jesus who felt hopelessly sad as he looked deep into the young man's soul and saw all he could have helped him become and the great things they could have achieved together.

What wouldn't we give to have three years travelling with Jesus, listening to him and watching him change people's lives? Yet Jesus saw what would stop this young man from becoming a famous apostle: he relied on his wealth to make him feel secure and worth something. I think that made Jesus feel disappointment and rejection.

I guess he feels the same about us when we rely on someone or something other than him for our sense of identity, purpose and security.

What holds you back from becoming the person Jesus longs for you to be? Your career, your gifting or the expectations of others? Is your identity vested in belonging to Jesus or are other things more important to you?

JENNIFER REES LARCOMBE

The unexpected sin

When Jesus saw him and knew he had been ill for a long time, he asked him, 'Would you like to get well?' 'I can't, sir,' the sick man said, 'for I have no one to put me into the pool.' (NLT)

I had been registered disabled, in a wheelchair, for six years and was supported by generous state benefits when, through the prayers of a new Christian, the Lord suddenly healed me in 1990. The massive change that healing made to my life was surprisingly stressful! I missed the company of all the kind people who had helped me, and I realised I would now have to earn my own living!

I've always wondered if the man who had been ill so long ever wondered how he would cope if he did manage to reach the pool first and all his charity handouts ceased. Also, whatever kind of sin could he possibly commit while lying there on his mat?

Maybe one of them was self-pity? Perhaps he often thought, 'It's not fair – no one helps me, I'm all alone and God never answers my prayers.' I remember, in my wheelchair days, often suffering with poor-old-me syndrome, or POMS as I called it. To be honest, I still have attacks of it now!

But is self-pity actually a sin? So many of us are prone to it. Yes, I believe it is. Like grumbling, it doubts and criticises God's care and provision and can be a way of manipulating others through guilt. Some people always like to cast themselves in the role of martyr, claiming, 'No one ever bothers to thank me for all I do behind the scenes at church,' or, 'Nothing ever goes right for me.'

It was complaining and discontent that kept all but two of the liberated slaves from ever reaching the promised land (Numbers 14:30).

The best cure for POMS during difficult situations seems to be to keep thanking the Lord for the small things that are actually good or going well (1 Thessalonians 5:18).

Lord, I'm so sorry I let myself think negatively about the circumstances you have allowed in my life. Help me recognise POMS the moment it begins to creep into my mind.

JENNIFER REES LARCOMBE

Practising what he preached

When they came to a place called The Skull, they nailed him to the cross. And the criminals were also crucified – one on his right and one on his left. Jesus said, 'Father, forgive them, for they don't know what they are doing.' (NLT)

There were several people here in hopeless situations, but only one realised it.

Just imagine the terrible punishment that those cruel, heartless soldiers would have received had Jesus not prayed for their forgiveness. What heartless, inhuman cruelty could inflict such torture on the Son of God himself – and think it was just part of a day's work. Imagine mutilating those hands that had done nothing but bring healing to the sick, nourishment to the hungry and comfort to the sorrowing. I often wonder if the forgiveness Jesus asked actually made it possible for them to come to faith in him at a later time in their lives. We may well meet them in heaven.

Perhaps the dying thief on the next cross overheard the words of Jesus and realised how desperately he also needed God's forgiveness. He too will be there in heaven. That promise of Jesus in verse 43 finally disproves the idea that it is our good works that get us to heaven – the thief never had time to do any!

Jesus said tantalisingly little about a lot of subjects but spoke often about forgiveness – perhaps because he puts such a high priority on it. In verse 34 we see him practising what he preached, in the midst of his agony.

We can feel that the little things people do to us which hurt are too small to need forgiveness, while major things are impossible to forgive. Yet failing to forgive even small things actually spoils our relationship with God and stunts our spiritual growth. Forgiving major things often does feel impossible, but when Jesus asks us to do something, he will always help us do it – if only we ask him.

One of the most healing prayers we can pray is, 'Lord, show me if there is anyone I need to forgive.' Sometimes it leads to God revealing a whole area of our past life that needs his healing touch.

JENNIFER REES LARCOMBE

'We had hoped...'

'He was a prophet, powerful in word and deed… Our rulers handed him over to be sentenced to death, and they crucified him; but we had hoped that he was the one who was going to redeem Israel.' (NIV)

Probably these two were typical of many followers of Jesus in Jerusalem that weekend. Perhaps they had once been healed or fed by Jesus, and their lives had been changed by his radical teaching. They had hoped he was the long-awaited Messiah, who would rid them of Roman occupation and make Israel great again, as it had been in the golden days of David and Solomon. All their hopes of freedom and prosperity had died with him at Golgotha. To those who had believed in his claims and promises, the crucifixion must have looked like the most hopeless situation in history. God had come to live with humankind on earth, but they had rejected him and tortured him to death.

As Jesus walked with Cleopas and his companion, he gave them a glimpse of God's big picture: his plan to make a permanent connection between himself and humankind – as well as making a welcome in heaven possible for those who chose to accept it.

How very wonderful that it was not only a theological sermon that Jesus preached to them, but he showed them that the heart of God's plan is for us to have loving, personal friendship with him. I can never read this story without crying with joy, as I picture them running back up to Jerusalem. They had not dared to let themselves hope that the women had been right – but now they knew for sure that Jesus was alive.

It is so easy for us to go through life looking up at the crushing problems that surround us. God wants us to look down on them from his perspective. Ephesians 2:6 tells us that God wants us to sit with him in the heavenly realms right now, not only in eternity.

Lord, I feel sure I will go through more hopeless situations in future, but help me to remember that your eyes are upon those 'whose hope is in your unfailing love' (Psalm 33:18).

JENNIFER REES LARCOMBE

Journeying into the promises of God: Joshua

Fiona Barnard writes:

I confess that this has been the most challenging set of notes I have written for *Day by Day with God*. Sitting in front of a computer in my comfortable home feels very different from marching into hostile territory to conquer it.

A summary of the book is contained in Moses' parting charge to Joshua: 'Be strong and courageous! For you will lead these people into the land that the Lord swore to their ancestors he would give them. You are the one who will divide it among them as their grants of land' (Deuteronomy 31:7, NLT). The book of Joshua tells us how it happened. As so often in scripture, theology is expressed through story. We are furnished with evidence of God's faithfulness in giving the long-promised land to a nomad people who were once slaves. We are shown the holiness of God in his concern for their wholehearted obedience to him and their shunning of evil Canaanite pagan practices. We are reminded of God's salvation in forming a covenant people, providing all they need in the face of powerful enemies. Foundational to Israel's understanding of itself is God's provision of the law, and now the land, so they may reflect his character to the world.

We cannot ignore the difficult issues. Our 21st-century sensibilities shudder at the military accounts of slaughter. Invasions and ethnic cleansing fill us with revulsion. Yet in Joshua, this does not seem to be a preoccupation. Rather there is a sense of awe at God's generosity and a passionate concern for the purity of his people. We need to look elsewhere, and in much greater detail, for ways to understand ancient 'holy war'.

Towering throughout this narrative is the man, Joshua, God's mouthpiece. Intent on fulfilling his God-given mandate and continuing the work Moses began, his wisdom is honed through experience and careful mentoring. He responds to God's instructions with faith and courage.

However, in these notes, I have chosen to focus more on the actions of the whole people of God because I think that speaks to all of us. Increasingly I am convinced that God works through teams, each of us using our gifts and wholehearted love to advance his kingdom. I pray that you may be surprised by what he will teach you through this, his word.

What's next?

'I will be with you… Be strong and courageous, because you will lead these people to inherit the land I swore to their ancestors to give them… Obey all the law… Meditate on it… Do not be afraid… for the Lord your God will be with you wherever you go.' (NIV)

I sat in church feeling wrung out. 'Are you excited?' asked the preacher, all teeth and cheeriness as he announced a new sermon series for a new term. 'We are going to be reading the book of Joshua and reflecting on the ways God leads his people.' After a rendition of the chorus 'Be bold, be strong', my feeling of dread tripled. I just wanted to be led to a dark room.

Then I noticed something that touched me. The opening of the book reads, 'After the death of Moses the servant of the Lord, the Lord said…' It struck me that these words were spoken with tenderness to a person in mourning. Joshua had lost a father figure, a wise mentor, an authoritative guide. They had worked and worshipped together; they had prayed and planned, led and laboured with God's people. Moses had been a bold intermediary, pleading directly with God for them and then conveying the divine will through the law in the years of wilderness wandering. There never was a miracle-working prophet like him. Now he was dead, leaving Joshua in charge. Abandoned on the edge of the promised land, Joshua and the people were grieving, overwhelmed and afraid.

And so I heard a whisper amid my own tumultuous feelings: 'I am with you. I go with you.' These are words of kindness, of understanding, of encouragement. 'I know the grief you are feeling. I see your fear and sense of inadequacy. So as you contemplate the challenges before you, look at me. Know I am with you. My promises and my word will hold you fast, if only you cling to me.' I may have heard all this before, but today, and each day, I am called afresh to trust.

'I will be with you': how might God's promise bring you courage and encouragement today?

FIONA BARNARD

Securing rest

'Your wives, your children and your livestock may stay in the land that Moses gave you east of the Jordan, but all your fighting men, ready for battle, must cross over… You are to help them until the Lord gives them rest, as he has done for you.' (NIV)

'You've been going around in circles in these hills long enough.' I was in the mountains of Wales when these words from Deuteronomy 2:2–3 hit me, but I knew God was not commenting on my hiking habits. I had drifted from paths of faithful obedience and was stumbling through valleys of doubt. Complaining, I felt angry and lost. Actually, I was also tired of tussling, very weary of wandering. And God said, 'Enough. Get on with it.' A wake-up call.

Through waywardness, God's people have trampled the long way round the wilderness for 40 years. Now God is saying, 'Enough. I will give you rest from your traveling. You will be able to unpack your bags, swap your tents for homes, plant seeds and stay long enough to watch fruit trees grow. But before you find your slippers, there are tough challenges ahead. You must be strong and courageous.' Two and a half of the twelve tribes already have their lands on the east of the River Jordan, but their possession is on the condition that they accompany and support their kin to secure their own lands. Now, as Joshua rallies the troops, they promise to sacrifice their time and safety for the sake of the whole people.

To a world of shattered billions, drained through injustice, persecution and strife, Jesus throws open his arms and cries, 'Come to me, all you who are weary and burdened, and I will give you rest' (Matthew 11:28). We who know him are invited to lean on him and draw on his life-giving Spirit. Then we are called to work with Christ in bringing good news to the desperate. Together as members of his body, we battle for fairness, integrity and peace. We discover the delight of rest in faithfulness, in fellowship, in following the one we love.

Today our battles most probably will not be physical ones. Nonetheless, how is Jesus calling you to demonstrate active solidarity with the needy?

FIONA BARNARD

Who would have thought?

'I know that the Lord has given this land to you… We have heard how the Lord dried up the water of the Red Sea… and what you did to Sihon… Our hearts sank… for the Lord your God is God in heaven above and on the earth below.' (NIV)

Wanted: preacher and encourager in strategic church position. Essential: watches the news, ponders its meaning, can negotiate and lie convincingly. Non-essential: moral, strong faith, full understanding of doctrine, part of the church.

I love this account of how the pagan Rahab became a vital member of God's holy people. Right at the beginning of a military history depicting battles and mayhem, we are ushered into the domestic domain of a prostitute's guest house. This lady goes well beyond the line of duty, but her instinct for survival and manipulation masks surprising theological insight. As travellers come and go through her 'hotel', she has been listening to tales of a foreign people who are doing amazing things. And somehow she has concluded that the agent powering this is not just a local deity, but the Lord of the whole earth. She is convinced beyond a shadow of a doubt that nothing will stand in his way. She and her city are destined to perish. 'I'll save you,' she whispers to the two spies sent to check things out in Jericho, 'but only if you will spare me and my family.'

So God works through this dubious character to protect them. There is more: he uses her prophetic, faith-filled words to assure his people of promises they had struggled so long to believe. The spies return relieved, but also triumphant: 'The Lord has surely given the whole land into our hands; all the people are melting in fear because of us' (v. 24).

Sometimes God's radical choice of personnel shocks us. We concoct a sane plan with sensible people and then – whoosh! – he scatters our criteria for divine headhunting to the wind. Amid the unpredictable and uncomfortable, he lifts our eyes to understand something new, through the most outrageous of messengers.

Lord, give me a sensitive heart today to note your care and protection even in the unexpected people, places and events.

FIONA BARNARD

Stepping out

'You will know that the living God is among you… See, the ark of the covenant of the Lord of all the earth will go into the Jordan… As soon as the priests who carry the ark… set foot in the Jordan, its waters flowing downstream will be cut off.' (NIV)

'What on earth am I doing here?' Dragged along by friends to an art retreat, I found myself staring helplessly at a brush and paints. As the leader read Psalm 66, I was struck by the image of God turning flowing water into dry land for his people to cross. Mixing blues and browns, I produced an infantile picture and wondered what this text had to do with me. However, soon the certainties in my life began to wobble: unexpected changes loomed over my house, job and church. Then I understood that God had assured me already of his presence. It made all the difference.

'The promised land is just over there,' God's people must have said as they camped by the river Jordan, 'so near and yet so far. How are we going to get across with our kids and grannies and tents?' The challenge of stepping out into a much-anticipated future is exciting but terrifying. So God calls them to prepare. This is not just a crossing: it is a holy moment. They are entering into God's purposes, which are weightier than their individual lives and luggage. This act changes history. They position themselves behind the ark, the symbol of God's presence. They follow the Lord of all the earth into the next stage of their journey with him. In doing it, they witness a miracle. Once again, as with their forebears leaving slavery in Egypt, the Lord parts the waters at just the right time. They cross on dry land. They have no doubt that the living God is with them in all their unknowns, and Joshua is his spokesperson.

In future years, the Israelites would celebrate this miracle. It would serve to remind them of God's personal leading even amid their less dramatic unknowns.

When we step out in obedience and faith, an unexpected event, a 'chance' conversation, a timely offer of prayer or, yes, even an art retreat, may strengthen us to press on for the love of Christ.

FIONA BARNARD

Building memories

'When your descendants ask their parents, "What do these stones mean?" tell them, "Israel crossed the Jordan on dry ground"… [God] did this so that all the peoples of the earth might know that the hand of the Lord is powerful and so that you might always fear the Lord your God.' (NIV)

What tricks do you have to help you remember things? A knot in your hanky? An alarm on your phone? Do you put notes on a calendar? What about preserving memories of past experiences? Do you take photos? Do you keep a scrapbook or a diary? Our daily lives are so full and interrupted, it is all too easy to overlook important things or forget them. Sometimes by default we fail to pay attention to what gives us life. Even miracles get swamped by the unrelenting need to keep going. The persistent tide of new challenges can swallow up our gratitude for God's sustaining hold on us.

God knows that the people of Israel will be secure and emboldened in their calling only as they recognise that he is all powerful. When they face trials, they must recall that fearing the Lord is more important than fearing the enemy. And so one person from each of the twelve tribes is asked to collect a stone from the very middle of the riverbed, recently covered with water, and carry it to the bank. These stones serve as evocative reminders of God's crucial intervention. They will trigger the curiosity of future generations who did not make the journey. They tell the story of the Lord's timely provision and his salvation.

Thank God for birthdays and anniversaries which prompt us to take stock and reflect. Those sentences with friends which begin 'Do you remember when…?' can make us smile. The measuring lines on doors charting a child's growth through the years evoke thanksgiving. Cards, objects, songs and places are all gifts to help us acknowledge God's grace in sorrow and struggle, solace and celebration.

How might you build prompts into your daily life to remind you of God's past and present goodness to you?

FIONA BARNARD

Eating faith

The day after the Passover... they ate some of the produce of the land: unleavened bread and roasted grain. The manna stopped the day after they ate this food from the land; there was no longer any manna for the Israelites, but that year they ate the produce of Canaan. (NIV)

I wish we did Thanksgiving in the UK – and not only for the turkey and pumpkin pie, the holiday or even the family gathering. Although I have never partaken in the real thing, I like the simple idea of gathering annually to make a special point of saying 'thank you'. I imagine joining a chorus through the centuries echoing gratitude for food, family and friends, harvest, home and health. I picture the faces of those I have loved around a table laden with goodies. I can almost hear them vocalise graces we so easily overlook in today's frenetic lifestyle: 'Today I am thankful for...'

Just think: after a lifetime of chewing only white manna for breakfast, dinner and tea, how would bread and lamb, green veg and herbs, honey, fruit and nuts feel in your mouth? Imagine the explosion of tastes and textures, colour and smell! After decades in the unforgiving harshness of desert living, the promises of harvest bounty would seem like heat-induced hallucination. But now God's people can pick and cook and savour God's goodness. They can enjoy his abundant provision and protection. They can celebrate, really celebrate, the feast of Passover, with all the side dishes. But centrally, they remember that the same Lord who delivered their ancestors from slavery in Egypt is finally bringing them home.

Just before this, the men were circumcised to signal their covenant obedience to God. Now in the context of this special relationship, the whole people pause to revel in his abundant care. They sing and tell stories, they eat and drink, they remember and pray, they laugh and cry. They say goodbye to manna and hello to God's future for them.

The Lord's supper provides a regular reminder of what Jesus has done for us. Together with brothers and sisters in Christ, we eat by faith with thanksgiving. But might there be a case for celebrating Thanksgiving in winter?

FIONA BARNARD

Holy ground

Now when Joshua was near Jericho, he looked up and saw a man standing in front of him with a drawn sword... Joshua went up to him and asked, 'Are you for us or for our enemies?' 'Neither,' he replied, 'but as commander of the army of the Lord I have now come.' (NIV)

A confession: I can't help it; even in my most spiritual moments, I detect a little voice whining in the background, 'What's in it for me?' In my prayers, I plead, 'Lord, please make it work out okay: not too much hassle or pain. Lots of joy won't go amiss. After all, you are my loving Father. Pleeease!'

So when I read these words, they hit home. Joshua sees a man with a sword. On the eve of a significant battle, his bottom line is, 'Are you for us or for our enemies?' After all, facing a long-awaited invasion, he needs to know. The response puts Joshua in his place: 'Neither. And this is holy ground, so take off your sandals.' Before anything else, Joshua is told to bow down before the God he is serving. In the rush to gear up for the fight, he must not overlook the sacred nature of his task. He is at the mercy of the divine army commander. It is the Lord's battle, not Joshua's.

Once on a retreat, I prayed, 'Lord, I want to take you with me next week. I would like you to meet my family, my students who come from all over the world to learn English, my colleagues in the office, the committee I serve at church, the friends who ring in the evening.' And as I visualised myself introducing Jesus to each one, I almost heard him say, 'No, I am not coming to see what you are doing for me. I am there already, because it is my work. Look for what I am doing in the lives of the people you think are yours.' It completely transformed my perspective. I am called to join what he is doing – in his way, for his purposes. Holy ground.

How might your prayers be different if you acknowledged God's holy purpose and presence in your projects long before you got involved?

FIONA BARNARD

God's battle

'Shout! For the Lord has given you the city!'… When the trumpets sounded, the army shouted, and at the sound of the trumpet, when the men gave a loud shout, the wall collapsed; so everyone charged straight in, and they took the city. They devoted the city to the Lord. (NIV)

'Joshua fought the battle of Jericho, and the walls came tumbling down.' I loved singing this song as a child, as I marched round the dining room table banging a saucepan with a spoon. Today, I am humming it again. Yet for all its familiarity, this is a very different world and I have many unanswerable questions: what were the Jericho inhabitants thinking as they watched a crowd trudging silently around their city for six days? How were the people feeling as they followed the ark of the covenant under the stares of their enemies? What was the effect of circling the city so many times? Who was most perplexed at the enthusiastic shouting on day seven?

However, certain points do stand out. In this book, accounts of conquest in the promised land begin with Jericho. Written by God's people, it tells of how the Lord fulfilled his ancient promise to give them their own land. The seven priests, seven trumpets, seven days and seven marches on the seventh day emphasise the religious nature of this campaign. The ark of the covenant, God's throne, is central. The text goes to great pains to underline that this is God's doing, through his power, for his purpose. And as if to put all that in neon-light capital letters, we are treated to the spectacle of this fortified city collapsing in a heap at the sound of a ragtag people worshipping the almighty God.

In our physical and spiritual battles, when we feel weak and overwhelmed, God's work must be done in his way. Fixing our eyes on Christ the King and fighting with the 'weapons' of truth, righteousness, gospel peace, faith, prayer and God's word will yield astonishing results in his alternative kingdom.

In the struggles you face, how might you 'be strong in the Lord and in his mighty power'? Read Ephesians 6:10–20 and imagine yourself putting on God's armour along with your brothers and sisters who march with you.

FIONA BARNARD

Holy gaze

'Israel has sinned; they have violated my covenant… They have stolen, they have lied, they have put them with their own possessions. That is why the Israelites cannot stand against their enemies… I will not be with you any more unless you destroy whatever among you is devoted to destruction.' (NIV)

'I want doesn't get,' my mother used to tell me when I asserted my seven-year-old human rights. For all the mantra of western individualism, no one is an island. A classmate doesn't own up to a misdemeanour, and everyone is punished. An irresponsible driver ignores a traffic light, and a family is killed. A megalomaniac ruler invites foreign sanctions, and all the people suffer. We are each affected by the desires and deeds of those around us. It isn't fair.

The story of Achan's sin is a challenge. The battle at Ai should have been straightforward, but the Israelites are soundly defeated. A devastated Joshua throws himself before God: after all his promises, how could Yahweh let this happen? 'Israel has broken the covenant,' comes the reply. In fact, it is not the whole people, but one man. Achan never imagined that his greed would have such drastic consequences: surely no one would notice him pilfering a beautiful robe, some silver and a bar of gold from an enemy household! Yet God did. This battle was not for personal gain, but for the establishment of God's holy people in that land and to rid it of evil. How then could there be disobedience, avarice, lying and stealing in the process? Achan's hidden selfishness is exposed to all the people and he is stoned to death with his family.

To our 21st-century sensibilities, this punishment seems unbelievably harsh. I cannot pretend to understand its significance as it was experienced then and recorded. What I do recognise is God's anger when we wander after materialistic idols, disregarding our promises to him and our community loyalty. Then he can do nothing with us; his good plans for us are damaged. The selfish 'I want' destroys all of us.

Are you conscious of sinful attitudes which affect your actions? Dare you bring them before God's holy gaze and ask for his forgiveness and strength?
FIONA BARNARD

From surrender to belonging

'Your servants have come from a very distant country because of the fame of the Lord your God. For we have heard reports of him… All those living in our country said to us, "… Go and meet them and say to them, 'We are your servants; make a treaty with us.'"' (NIV)

What do you make of that? Our journey with the Israelites makes interesting and sometimes puzzling reading! This story is one example. In our engagement with the Bible we have to be honest and admit that we are slightly baffled by or fail to understand some of the tales we read. A dose of humility does not go amiss, along with some research and imagination!

On the face of it, this appears to be an account of how the Gibeonites, who were next on the list of groups to conquer, tricked God's people into making a peace treaty. They claimed to have come from far away. Presented with worn-out shoes and mouldy bread, the Israelites trusted the evidence of their eyes and noses, rather than consulting the Lord. Consequently, they were bound to their promise.

However, there are parallels with the earlier story of Rahab, who also lied to save her skin. In my struggle with the stories of destruction, it offers a beacon of hope. For this is another explanation of how near neighbours are not obliterated, but incorporated into the life and, significantly, the worship of God's people. Before this almighty God, all they can do is submit as servants to the people among whom he dwells. Their surrender results in a new calling to be 'woodcutters and water-carriers for the assembly, to provide for the needs of the altar of the Lord' (v. 27). It is also where they will be given the opportunity to know of his goodness and care.

Recently, I spoke to someone who has begun attending church: 'I feel so much better after I have been!' She may still not be a believer, but she is attracted to this community where she feels she is accepted. Jesus is drawing her to himself.

Watch for the people who 'come around' your church. Are there further ways you can help them feel they belong, participate in activities and understand more about Jesus?

FIONA BARNARD

Wholehearted

'Here I am today, eighty-five years old!… I'm just as vigorous to go out to battle now as I was then. Now give me this hill country that the Lord promised me… The Lord helping me, I will drive them out just as he said.' (NIV)

Age is a funny thing. Some people seem ancient in their 40s, often struggling with physical and mental challenges. Others boast of tackling marathons and mountains at an age when they could be expected to be rocking in chairs by the fire.

Caleb is among the marathon men! At 85 years old, he is still keen to fight God's battles. The job remains unfinished and he is taking no rest until it is. But is Caleb simply a lucky arthritis-free octogenarian, or is there more to his story? The few details we have paint a picture of a man full of faith, utterly devoted to God. Forty-five years earlier, when his fellow spies terrified the people by reporting giants in the land who would defeat them, Caleb championed trust in the Lord who would give them victory. Enduring four decades of wasteful wilderness wandering, as a result of their disobedience, must have been a huge frustration for this man of action and faith. Yet when the time comes, he is ready. He is passionate. He is still excited by what God can do through him and relies on his help. His wholehearted commitment to God's cause is inspirational.

'Christians don't retire!' was my parents' watchword as they approached their mid-60s and sought the Lord's guidance for all that followed until they died. It was tough acknowledging they were less energetic and more forgetful. They did have to keep adjusting their activities. But they did not retire from following Jesus wholeheartedly and being involved in his work through prayer and encouragement. Looking through their correspondence recently, I was challenged on rediscovering the key to their passion: 'Christ's love compels us' (2 Corinthians 5:14). As I have pondered my own future, my prayer has been, 'Lord, increase my love for you!', because I realise that everything follows from that.

What challenges are you facing? God of Caleb, enlarge my faith and give me strength to be wholehearted in the pursuit of your purposes for my life. Increase my love for you.

FIONA BARNARD

Bridge across the river

'We will worship the Lord at his sanctuary with our burnt offerings…
"Look at the replica of the Lord's altar, which our ancestors built, not
for burnt offerings and sacrifices, but as a witness between us and
you." Far be it from us to rebel against the Lord.' (NIV)

'I do love Jesus. It's his family I don't like.' I know so many believers for
whom petty church squabbles have fostered disillusionment and dis-
enchantment with the institution.

War threatens the union of Israel. Once all the tribes were settled, Joshua
sent the clans of Reuben, Gad and Manasseh home to their families east of
the Jordan with thanks and God's blessing. They had fought alongside their
brother tribes, even though they already had their own land. But suddenly,
the solidarity and union of the Israelites looks set to be destroyed with
news that they have built an altar by the Jordan. High priest Phinehas goes
with tribal representatives to talk face to face. In the meeting, he expresses
alarm that another altar will compromise worship, deviating from God's
prescribed way and place. He voices the fear that it will imperil the mission
of the whole people to be holy and wholly devoted to God.

In response, Phinehas is assured that covenant faithfulness is precisely
why the altar has been erected: it is a visual reminder for succeeding generations that the river cannot divide them. Together they belong to God's
covenant people.

After a particularly agonising time of argument and accusation in my
church, the arrival of a new pastor heralded a ceasefire. He was a gifted
peacemaker. I watched what he did: instead of blasting off another email
and storing replies as evidence, he knocked on doors and listened to all
parties. Tirelessly, he pursued a peace which did not ignore the issues, but
heard the concerns underlying them. His disarming manner and prayer-
fulness enabled God's healing to touch each of us and brought a unity we
could never have imagined. A stagnant, broken church began to see new
life and the baptistry open for kingdom business.

---

*When Christians are so weakened and distracted by division and distrust,
how might you be a bridge-builder and a peacemaker?*

FIONA BARNARD

When all is said and done...

'The Lord your God fights for you... So be very careful to love the Lord your God... Now I am about to go the way of all the earth. You know with all your heart and soul that not one of all the good promises the Lord your God gave you has failed.' (NIV)

What is it all about? Dismantling my parents' home has been a sobering exercise. I have spent a lot of time in a memory labyrinth, as clothes and photos, letters and objects have triggered recollections of meals, trips and relationships. Amid the nostalgia, however, has been the challenge to consider my own life, my priorities and my purpose. When it has all been said and done, what will my three score years and ten (or more) finally say and do?

As Joshua approaches his own death, he pours out his heart: all that has moved and motivated him. This is not to secure a legacy but because, as Israel's leader for so many years, he longs more than anything that God's will be done in them and through them. He takes Israel's leaders on a tour of their recent history, reminding them of all that God has done in driving out their enemies and giving them a homeland. He voices his confidence in the Lord for all that he will do to ensure they are safe and secure. I imagine his tone becomes graver as he reiterates the divine deal. This is all part of God's much bigger plan that they reflect his holy character in community: obeying his law, having nothing to do with the pagan worship of their neighbours, demonstrating loyalty and loving him alone.

You know, Joshua, all these centuries later, you are spot on! As I wade through parental diaries and archives, unearthing secrets and unpacking explanations, I cling to this: the Lord is true. He has been faithful in my family's earthly pilgrimage. And as I face a strangely empty future, I am rediscovering a passion to know and love Jesus, because at the end of the day, it is all that counts.

'Love the Lord your God': Lord, please help me, my family and my church to love you today.

FIONA BARNARD

Choose today...

'Choose for yourselves this day whom you will serve, whether the gods your ancestors served beyond the Euphrates, or the gods of the Amorites, in whose land you are living. But as for me and my household, we will serve the Lord.' (NIV)

Do you like history? Does the word conjure up boring dates and unpronounceable names, distant heroes and remote events? Well, today's reading takes us on a selected history of Israel to lift our gaze beyond the here and now to God's patient story-making. So often we feel that things occur beyond our planning or doing or desiring. Yet this account encourages us to trace God's masterful hand beyond the happenings of our days to his loving sovereign design. If we are in his family, we are part of his bigger picture, even if we are too close to see it now.

As the elderly Joshua assembles all the tribes, he underlines God's initiative in calling them to be his people. God picked the childless Abraham to be a father. He chose Moses to rescue their ancestors from slavery. He fought for them and gave them the land he had promised Abraham. He ensured Balaam blessed them, rather than cursed them, despite Barak's instructions. The Lord did all this. Now they have to decide: who will they serve? That is the challenge which comes again and again to them: how will you respond?

Our journey with Joshua and God's people has felt very alien to our own. Yet that word 'serve', repeated here many times, is utterly relevant for us: in view of all that God has done in your life and in the history of your community, how will you respond? Joshua understands that we cannot answer nonchalantly off the cuff. This demands everything of us: faith, hard slog, sacrifice. We who live this side of the cross know what Jesus has accomplished for us. We have the Holy Spirit to keep us faithful. So we can say, 'By God's amazing grace, we will serve the Lord.'

Draw a timeline of your life or that of your faith community. Include the high and low points. How has God been faithful? What is your response?

FIONA BARNARD

Journey to the cross

Hannah Fytche writes:

Have you ever seen the four symbols of the lion, the eagle, the ox and the man, painted or carved as decorations on old churches? Or perhaps in ancient illuminated manuscripts? In the centre of my city there are statues of them on the four corners of a church tower.

Each represents one of the gospel writers: the man for Matthew, the ox for Luke, the lion for Mark and the eagle for John. John is the eagle because eagles can look straight at the sun without blinking; John, in his gospel, looks straight at Christ and the Father, seemingly without blinking. His writing contains so much rich theology and brilliant truth about Jesus that it is dazzlingly bright: 'The light shines in the darkness,' he writes, 'and the darkness has not overcome it' (John 1:5, NIV).

As we travel through the last days of Lent and into the Holy Week of Easter, I invite you to look with me at the light John finds on Jesus' journey to the cross. What mysteries can we find in Jesus' words about his purpose on earth and his relationship with the Father? How does Jesus reveal the Father to us? Let's follow Christ's light through the dark days of doubt and contention which surrounded his life and death and hear the words he says to us about who he really is. Let's expect to be enlightened as God speaks through these words to our lives today. Let's be brought to our knees in worship as we glimpse more of God's glory and brilliance, and let's be raised to our feet in the strength he gives us to continue following him.

As we reach Holy Week, you will find that the readings don't match up with each day – for example, you will find the story of Jesus washing his disciples' feet a few days before Maundy Thursday (when the church calendar remembers this event). This is so that we have time to go slowly over the events and words of Jesus in the last days before his death. Go slowly, for this is holy ground, and God has much to say.

Pray as we begin. Lift to God the darkness of contention and doubt that perhaps surrounds or is within your own life. Ask for his light to guide and strengthen you.

Let us journey to the cross.

Son revealing Father

No one has ever seen God, but the one and only Son, who is himself God and is in the closest relationship with the Father, has made him known. (NIV)

No one has ever seen God, John testifies.

Sometimes we talk about seeing God in creation: in the burning colours of sunset or the startling beauty of a kingfisher's wing. You might see God on the streets, in the wise or tired eyes of people around you. You might hear him speaking to you in the music of a choir or band or through the words of a well-preached sermon. I often see God in the words that I read, in the poetry of G.M. Hopkins, Mary Oliver and George Herbert; in academic tomes and Bible commentaries; in good stories that tell the truth.

We say we see God in so many ways. Yet *no one* has ever seen God, John writes. No one has ever *seen* him.

We have not stood face to face with the almighty, overwhelmed by his expansive glory, by his incredible power and love. We have no words to express what this would be like, because we have never experienced it. We couldn't. God the Father, in all glory, is removed from us. Untouchable. Unseen.

No one has ever seen God, John writes, *but* (hallelujah!) the one and only Son has made him known. The Son makes the Father known. He makes the invisible visible, the untouchable tangible, the overwhelming comprehensible. He is the exact image and likeness of his Father: he embodies – enfleshes, enacts – the love at the centre of God's being. In the Son, God becomes flesh and dwells among us. He is Emmanuel, God with us.

So have you ever seen God?

We see him in Jesus, his Son. John testifies to this in the prologue of his gospel and will go on to show us how Jesus, during his life, death and resurrection, reveals the Father.

There are no words to describe what it would be like to see God. Spend five minutes in complete silence. Pray, wait, listen. If it helps, repeat this phrase as a way of focusing your prayer: 'Lord Jesus Christ, Son of God.'

HANNAH FYTCHE

First glimpse

'Everyone brings out the choice wine first and then the cheaper wine after the guests have had too much to drink; but you have saved the best till now.' What Jesus did here in Cana of Galilee was the first of the signs through which he revealed his glory. (NIV)

Jesus celebrates with his friends at a wedding. You probably know the story: the wine runs out, and Mary calls Jesus over to solve this – clearly very serious – problem. I love this story's sparkling humour: the Son of God is called by his mum to turn water into wine.

You can imagine the expression in Mary's and Jesus' eyes: perhaps it's a laughing expression, glimmering with some delightful secret. 'There's no more wine,' Mary states, and I think Jesus would've laughed back: 'Woman – *mum* – why do you involve me now? It's not yet my time!'

Yet Mary knows Jesus will provide. 'Do whatever he tells you,' she says to the servants, her eyes smilingly fixed on Jesus. She knows he will pour exquisite joy into this celebration. She knows that Jesus doesn't do things by halves. She knows that he reveals his Father's heart: his Father's generous, caring heart.

Jesus turns to the servants and they fill jars with water. The banquet-master tastes the water and exclaims with delight over the quality of the wine. Did the servants see the moment when it changed? Did Jesus wink at Mary as he transformed clear aqua into finest vintage? Did his disciples, believing in him, pass him skins of water for days afterwards, daring him to do it again, to recreate the miracle?

Who knows? But what we do know – what we do see of Jesus and of the Father through him – is that God is generous; he gives in abundance; he celebrates with his people, including you and me! In John's gospel Jesus' earthly ministry begins with a party and feast. This looks towards the heavenly feast that God is preparing, and it transforms our varied present moments into places where God can bring joy.

How wonderful a first glimpse of the adult Jesus this is!

Jesus, thank you that you are joyful; you delight to give me joy. In the midst of whatever is happening, cause me to celebrate the life you've given me and the love you have for me. Make me dance even in the downpour.

HANNAH FYTCHE

Resistance to the light

'I am the bread of life. Whoever comes to me will never go hungry, and whoever believes in me will never be thirsty. But as I told you, you have seen me and still you do not believe.' (NIV)

At the time of writing, I have just moved into a new house with three people I'm only just getting to know – two of whom I've only just met. We're learning to live as a community alongside our placements in churches in our city. One thing that has made this transition time easier is the bread-maker that one of my housemates, Naomi, brought with her.

We make 'Naomi bread' every few days, adding yeast first, then flour, followed by sugar and salt, water and oil, and a couple of handfuls of seeds. 'Naomi bread' is a staple of our newly formed household, bringing sustenance and joy.

Jesus says to a crowd of curious followers that he is the bread of life. He's just fed 5,000 people on a mountainside with fish and bread (vv. 1–14). Now he's explaining what it means for him to be the bread of life, their sustenance and joy.

Come to me, he says, and feast on all the good gifts I give you, from the breath you breathe to the relationships you enjoy to the vision of heaven I inspire you with. Come to me, and you will find life to sustain you through each and every moment.

Later, Jesus breaks bread and shares it as a symbol of the life for all that will come through his death. Come to me, he says, because I am broken for you. I am the bread of your life.

Jesus says all of this – and, incredibly, some of his listeners grumble. They don't understand how Jesus can be 'bread from heaven', sent by God. Jesus reveals who he is, and they don't see it: they resist the light he is shining on his identity and purpose. Let us not do the same.

Let us instead receive the torn bread he offers us. Let us taste and see that he is good.

Jesus, you endure resistance to the revelation of who you are. Give me understanding to know you as the bread of my life: my sustenance and my joy. Open my eyes that I may see. Open my hands that I may receive.

HANNAH FYTCHE

Opening eyes to see

After saying this, [Jesus] spat on the ground, made some mud with the saliva, and put it on the man's eyes. 'Go,' he told him, 'wash in the Pool of Siloam' (this word means 'Sent'). So the man went and washed, and came home seeing. (NIV)

'The man went and washed, and came home seeing.' Sit with those words; mull them over. Aren't they astonishing?

Jesus – the bread of life, the one who brings the wine to the party, the Son who makes the Father known – spits on earth and rubs the resultant mud in a blind man's eyes. The man goes to a pool and washes the mud, made by Jesus, out from his eyes. The water runs down his face, and he begins to see colours and shapes all around him. Light sparkles off the pool's surface, and this is the first time he's seen it: ordinary light sparkling off an ordinary pool becomes most extraordinary when seen by a once-blind man.

Jesus opens blind eyes so that they see ordinary, extraordinary things. In verses 35–37 we see that Jesus opened the blind man's eyes not only to see light and water and colour, but also so that he could see Jesus. 'You have now seen him – the Son of Man,' Jesus says. You have seen the man who uses ordinary mud to communicate his message, the extraordinary Son who bears the image and likeness of his Father. 'You have seen God,' Jesus tells him.

In our journey towards the cross, we are seeing that Jesus makes himself known in the ordinary lives of everyday people. So instead of merely claiming to see, like the Pharisees (9:39–41), let us seek, like the once-blind man, to see with our eyes opened wide by Jesus.

Let us seek, see and find that Christ is present in ten thousand places: he is present in the ordinary stuff of bread, wine, mud and our own human experience. He is present in all of life, and he transforms all to become an extraordinary place and opportunity to know him: a place where light sparkles off the surface of the pool and off the surface of our lives and astonishes us with its beauty as if for the very first time.

Jesus, thank you that you opened the eyes of the blind. Thank you that you open my eyes. Let me not claim to see well without really seeing you. Let me see you in my everyday experiences, knowing you increasingly.

HANNAH FYTCHE

Raising Lazarus to life

When he had said this, Jesus called in a loud voice, 'Lazarus, come out!' The dead man came out, his hands and feet wrapped with strips of linen, and a cloth round his face. Jesus said to them, 'Take off the grave clothes and let him go.' (NIV)

Two summers ago I travelled to Rome with friends. One blisteringly hot day we trekked across a national park to visit catacombs: networks of underground passageways in which early Christians, hiding even their dead from persecuting powers, were buried. I ventured into the first tour-guided catacomb, feeling the temperature plummet and seeing how easy it would be to get lost. Each passageway was lined with narrow shelf-like graves.

While my friends continued on a second tour, I stayed above ground in warm sunlight. Leading away from the catacombs' entrance, alongside a pathway of Italian cypresses, was a series of carvings. I followed the path and realised that the carvings told the stories of Jesus' resurrection appearances.

Il risorto si mostra ai discepoli; the risen one shows himself to the disciples. *Il risorto in cammino con i discepoli di Emmaus*; the risen one walking with the disciples of Emmaus. *Il risorto si manifesto nello spezzare il pane*; the risen one manifests in the breaking of the bread. *Il risorto, il risorto, il risorto*. The risen one, the risen one, the risen one.

Jesus is the risen one. In the dark days leading to his death he showed that the grave does not contain him: his living footsteps will lead away from the entrance of the tomb. Jesus is the risen one and the *raising* one: he speaks, and Lazarus' body reanimates; a dead man comes to life.

Jesus speaks, and we come to life, leaving dead things in our lives – broken things, secret things, painful things, shameful things – behind us. All that holds us back from living is cast aside by Jesus' voice: 'Take off the grave clothes,' he commands, and go. Live. Be.

Jesus speaks, and we can step out into sunlight, feel warmth on our skin, blink away the sleep of death. We can breathe again. Hallelujah.

Jesus, you are the risen one. I celebrate that your footsteps lead away from the grave. Help me to see the things in my life into which you long to breathe new life and new hope. Breathe life there: I cry out to you for life.

HANNAH FYTCHE

Jesus predicts his death

'Very truly I tell you, unless a grain of wheat falls to the ground and dies, it remains only a single seed. But if it dies, it produces many seeds.' (NIV)

A seed falls to theground. Dirt and soil cover it. It slowly bursts in darkness. It dies. It breaks. It breaks *open*, as new life pushes out. It grows, stem forging bravely through earth into air. Soon enough it produces many more seeds. But first it had to fall.

This is the image by which Jesus reveals himself, at a festival, in response to those who want to see him. The image by which they are invited to see Jesus is an image of life to death – a seed falling and breaking – and death to life – a seed breaking open and growing to produce more seeds.

It's incredible that God, become man, reveals himself like this. God's pattern is startling – it is life to death to life. Through Jesus' death, life emerges: life for many; life for the world.

This sacrifice – this willingness to fall, die and be covered by darkness – is the essence of God's love for us in Christ. Dwell with that for a while…

Jesus reveals that God's love is so immense that he is willing for his own self to break, to be shattered, to be rent and torn, to be killed.

It is even more striking because Jesus reveals to his seekers at the festival that he chooses this sacrifice, through a great internal battle. 'My soul is troubled, and what shall I say? "Father, save me from this hour"? No, it was for this very reason I came to this hour. Father, glorify your name!' (vv. 27–28). Christ's willingness cost him dearly. God's love for us cost God dearly.

Carry that image of a seed with you. Plant a seed and watch it break open and grow, as a reminder of Christ's sacrifice, driven by love. This is your God.

Jesus, impress on my heart something of your immense pattern of life to death and death to life. Give me an understanding of your costly sacrifice, that I may allow my own life to break open to share your love with the world.
HANNAH FYTCHE

97

Servant Son

Jesus knew that the Father had put all things under his power, and that he had come from God and was returning to God; so he got up from the meal, took off his outer clothing, and wrapped a towel round his waist. (NIV)

Christ, in the knowledge that all things, even life and death, had been given into his power, wraps a towel round his waist and washes dirt from hardened toes. The extraordinary Christ reveals himself in ordinary water and soap, in an act of self-giving love. God kneels to wash the feet of humankind.

In response, I claim Simon Peter's first reaction: 'Lord, are you going to wash my feet?' Lord, Christ, Creator-King – are you going to wash *my* feet? Are you going to humble yourself to the hard-work task of washing and cleaning, while I just sit here and be? Are you going to stoop to touch and even smell my feet, to experience my life's grit and sorrow? I can't believe that you would bring heaven so low and close to my earthly existence. I can't believe it; help my unbelief.

How often do you question Christ's deeply loving and wholly good intentions towards you? How often do you not understand that your God is a self-giving God, acting by love?

'You do not realise now what I am doing,' Jesus replies to Simon Peter, 'but later you will understand.'

Bring before Jesus Christ your sorrows and your dirt-smudged feet. Bring to him your fears and the things that you hide away. Dare to let him touch you, scrub away the pain and hardness of your weary living. See that he wants to give himself to you. Be made free by his love.

Write down those hidden things, speak them aloud to Christ, then perhaps confess them to a friend you trust. There's power to heal in the voicing and naming of what you hide: Jesus is gentle as he brings your feet to the washbasin and cleans away that which holds you back from him, that which holds you back from fully living.

Jesus Christ, you are the holy God who washes feet. Help me to trust you as I dare to bring to you my feet, sorrows, shame. I come with the weariness of carrying that which weighs me down. Wash me, that I might live.

HANNAH FYTCHE

The way to the Father

'Do not let your hearts be troubled. You believe in God; believe also in me. My Father's house has many rooms; if that were not so, would I have told you that I am going there to prepare a place for you?' (NIV)

In the swirling, contentious darkness surrounding Jesus during his last days on earth, John writes that Jesus comforts his disciples. He gives them truth for standing firm in the days to come. He has knelt to wash their feet; he has predicted Peter's denial; he has seen Judas hurry into the night. Then he whispers to them, 'Do not let your hearts be troubled.' Those hard-beating pulses, quickened by fear of what will happen – let them even now be quiet, untroubled.

Is your heart ever troubled? You live in a world in which doubt, fear and confusion are prevalent – much like the night of Jesus' betrayal. In this world, what is it that you worry about? Do you ever feel like there isn't enough light by which to see the road ahead? Sometimes living can feel like a constant mustering of enough trust and courage to move your feet forwards, even in darkness. Living sometimes requires a lot of bravery.

Jesus kindles bravery within us as he whispers to us, his disciples, 'Do not let your hearts be troubled.' Even here, on the edge of paths unknown, let your heart be quiet.

Do not let your heart be troubled because Jesus, God-become-man, *reveals* the way to God the Father (vv. 9–10). Jesus lights up the road. He does not allow our hearts to be troubled because he knows and shows us the way to the one who holds our hearts, gives us all we need and prepares a room for us in his place, his heart.

It's like a shaft of light piercing dark night. Through it all – even through those last, holy, painful days leading to his death, even through our own holy and painful days – Jesus illuminates the way to the Father.

Do not let your heart be troubled.

Jesus, even when I see darkness around me, you are there. The darkness is not dark to you; the night will shine like the day (Psalm 139:11–12). May this truth enlighten my heart, strengthening me to continue.

HANNAH FYTCHE

Vine and branches

'You did not choose me, but I chose you and appointed you so that you might go and bear fruit – fruit that will last – and so that whatever you ask in my name the Father will give you. This is my command: love each other.' (NIV)

We dwelt yesterday on how Jesus illuminates the way to the Father. We know too that Jesus calls his disciples, us, to 'shine', so that we illuminate the way for others. In Matthew (5:14–16) we are called cities on a hill: beacons of light beckoning all people to come and see God.

Sometimes we talk about ourselves as light using the language of reflection. Jesus is the light; we are not. Therefore we *reflect* his light, like a mirror reflects lamplight or like the moon reflects sunlight. While this is true, today's reading shows us that we are not as passive as a mirror or the moon. We are not separate from Jesus, surfaces off which his light bounces; amazingly, today's reading shows us that we are as intimately connected to him as a branch is to its vine.

Imagine the part of a plant where a branch or leaf connects to the stem. If you are near a plant, go look. Can you see where the leaf or branch joins? It's a confluence of two living parts. Picture the insides of that joining point. There are myriad upon myriad cells there, passing energy between themselves so that the plant may grow and bear fruit. The stem energises the leaves, and the leaves the stem.

Jesus says that he chooses us to bear fruit. He says that we are the branches, and he is the vine. Like a branch is joined to the vine, so we are joined to Jesus. The same power that raised him from the dead lives in us.

When I am worn out by remaining faithful to what God's calling me to do, I remember that I am joined to Christ as a branch is joined to a vine. This strengthens me, and I can continue.

Jesus, be near me in this moment. Show me how close you are to me: as close as a vine is to one of its own branches. I praise you that you choose me to participate in your life, strengthening me always with your power.

HANNAH FYTCHE

Jesus prays

'Holy Father, protect them by the power of your name, the name you gave me, so that they may be one as we are one.' (NIV)

I am writing this the day after the December 2019 UK general election. I don't know where we will be as a nation in March 2021, but, at time of writing, a prayer for unity from the lips of Jesus brings me to my knees.

Jesus, having comforted his disciples, kneels in the last hours of his life and prays for his people's unity with each other and with God. Around him swirls political and religious contention; his experience in the world resists visions of unity, even among believers. Darkness compels him to a passionate plea: 'I am not praying for the world, but for those you have given me, for they are yours' (v. 9). *Make your people one, Father.*

Where do you see discord in church community? Maybe there is destructive tension within your local church, a wound still open with unforgiveness. Maybe there is a split due to difference of opinion, theology or practice. The global church has been fragmented for centuries into different theologies and traditions, often too fiercely defended. My heart aches.

My heart aches, and it is in this prayer of Jesus Christ that I find hope. On Jesus' heart is concern for people's unity. He knows that divisions will occur and that fractures will splinter friend from friend and parent from child. He falls to his knees and prays to the Father for the protection of his people: 'Protect them by the power of your name.' He goes to the cross for the sake of reconciliation.

It astounds me that we get to eavesdrop on this conversation. We are privileged to listen to God's intimate heartbeat, Christ's deep desires for his creation. It reassures me that Jesus allows us to hear specifically his cry for unity. It holds me close and keeps me going when world and church fragment.

Jesus, as you prayed to make your people one, so I join you in that prayer. Give me your wisdom to discern how to heal and reconcile friend with friend and parent with child. Give me courage and sensitivity to act on this wisdom.
HANNAH FYTCHE

Arrested

Jesus commanded Peter, 'Put your sword away! Shall I not drink the cup the Father has given me?' (NIV)

The setting is a garden, like the first setting for humankind described in Genesis 1—2. A garden: the place where, both times, the creator dwells with his people and is betrayed by them. A shadow hovers over this place; and yet darkness does not prevail.

In the garden of John 18, Jesus Christ shines in shadow's midst. He illuminates his arresters with knowledge of who he is – 'Jesus of Nazareth' – so that they draw back and fall to the ground (v. 6). He shines brightly with scripture's fulfilment, demonstrating that even this dark moment is held within God's purposes (v. 9). He blazes with the glory of the Son as he submits, in that darkest hour, to his Father's will (v. 11).

This is how Jesus appears to me in this passage: as one standing in the middle of swirling darkness holding out a powerful, steady light.

As uncertainty and fear descend, Peter lashes out with a sword. Maybe if the soldiers, the visible symbol and immediate cause of the fear, are injured, then darkness will flee. Peter is wrong: violence does not cast out darkness. Conflict does not subdue fear.

Christ shows us that light casts out darkness. Trust in his Father's love casts out fear. He reprimands Peter: 'Put your sword away! Shall I not drink the cup the Father has given me?' (v. 11). Christ's light is that of confidence in his Father's will. The Son submits to arrest because his Father, who is good and who loves him, has given him this task.

Dwell with this image of Jesus Christ. Try, impossible as it is, to imagine how he felt. Be strengthened by his example: your God knows how you feel when you face darkness. God knows what it means and how much it costs you to choose to trust his love.

Jesus Christ, you stood in that garden and felt fear descend around you, yet you stood firm in the confidence of God's goodness. May I do the same: increase my trust, that I may respond to darkness with light.

HANNAH FYTCHE

Sentenced

The Jewish leaders insisted, 'We have a law, and according to that law he must die, because he claimed to be the Son of God.' (NIV)

Contention climaxes in this scene of Jesus' sentencing. This is where surrounding darkness descends sharply: a crown of thorns is pushed on to his head and digs into his scalp; the sarcastic words of his mocking opponents lash out to sting the soul.

The religious leaders identify their problem with Jesus: 'He claimed to be the Son of God.' This claim, which in us provokes praise, provokes in the leaders of the time a violent outcry. The light of the world is bound with instruments of darkness – thorns and mockery. The King is made into a parody of himself by those who disbelieve and feel threatened by him.

'Take him away! Take him away! Crucify him!' they cry (v. 15).

It is easy to want to skim over this moment. We might want to briefly acknowledge that darkness bound Jesus – but we probably don't want to dwell with that image. It is too much, too painful. Yet the binding of darkness around the light of God's Son is part of the story written by God (v. 11). It is important that we pause here: what reaction rises up within you as you read this passage?

I find comfort as well as pain. It is a powerful image: I am astonished that Jesus submitted himself to this end for the sake of a new beginning for his world – for creation, us, you, me.

When I am discouraged by my weakness – by loneliness, fear or doubt – this is an image to which I can turn, knowing that it will break my heart open both to sorrow and to new confidence: sorrow which moves me to my knees; confidence which raises me to my feet again, in the strength of Christ's indescribable love displayed in the sacrifice he made.

Jesus, draw near and help me to know the cost of your sacrifice, that it may open my eyes to your love. Break my heart over the sin of the world which led you to this moment. May I move from this place with your new life.

HANNAH FYTCHE

Crucified, dead and buried

When he had received the drink, Jesus said, 'It is finished.' With that, he bowed his head and gave up his spirit. (NIV)

The Son chose to submit to his Father's will: 'Shall I not drink this cup the Father has given me?' (18:11). Now we see this submission. Jesus receives death's bitter drink.

He drinks wine vinegar from a sponge and gives up his spirit. His body is broken; his side is pierced. Lifeless, he is removed from the cross and buried in a cave. He is literally laid in the darkness of the earth. Light is extinguished.

When you hear the words 'Do this in remembrance of me', spoken in a Communion or Eucharist service, what do you remember? Do you remember Jesus sitting with his disciples at Passover, offering them food and drink? Do you remember Jesus meeting and calling people with joy? Do you remember Christ's broken body, laid in the tomb?

There are many moments that Communion calls us to remember, moments which form us as we recall how Jesus makes us part of his story. Around Easter, I sometimes recall this moment: Jesus receiving the drink and then giving up his spirit.

Jesus receives a bitter drink – and I take the cup of sweet wine, resonant with the gift of life.

Jesus says that it is finished – and I hear the words at the end of the service, 'Go in peace to love and serve the Lord', and know that my life is always being made new.

Jesus gives up his spirit – and I feel my spirit enlivened by his presence and give all that I can to love and serve the Lord.

In this darkest moment of Jesus' death are seeds of new life. Jesus' body breaks so that we are made whole; he breathes his last so that we breathe our first. This Good Friday, our memory of Christ's bitter cup can become for us the cup of life.

Jesus, I praise you. I worship you. I delight in you, because you have made it possible for me to have life. Thank you for drinking the bitter cup of death. May I always drink the sweet cup of life with devotion and gratefulness in my heart.
HANNAH FYTCHE

Let there be light

The light shines in the darkness, and the darkness has not overcome it. (NIV)

In the grieving of Easter Saturday, we call to mind our hopes and fears. Jesus Christ is crucified, dead and buried. All that we have seen and heard of him, and of the God from whom he comes, is buried with him. In the darkness lies our dying glimpses of his life. Love is extinguished.

Or so it seems.

Let us remember those glimpses. We've seen Jesus' miracles. We've heard him talk about himself as a seed that must die to bring more life. We've eavesdropped on his prayer to the Father. We've wondered at Christ's submission to being bound by darkness – and we've been inspired by his trust in his Father.

We recall the words at the start of John's gospel: 'The light shines in the darkness, and the darkness has not overcome it' (v. 5).

In the grieving of Easter Saturday, then, we call to mind our hopes, and they eclipse our fears. Even though Christ is dead, he will rise again, like a plant growing from a buried seed, like light shining in darkness.

We hope and trust that there will be light. Please God, let there be light.

This trust and hope are not just for Easter Saturday. Hope must endure in all dark times while we wait for Jesus to come again.

On the day that my grandad died, I found myself proclaiming this message in the middle of a worship meeting. I hadn't planned this – but when the invitation came for anyone to pray or share encouragement from the microphone, I found myself at the front before I'd had a chance to think.

'In this world we are all going to face hard things,' I spoke, 'yet in Jesus there is hope that conquers even death. Light shines in the darkness, and the darkness will never overcome it.'

Please, God, let there be light: in all places, at all times, for all people. Let your dawn from on high break upon us. Let the dawn of Easter Sunday come with healing in its rays.

HANNAH FYTCHE

Resurrection

Nell Goddard writes:

I'll be honest with you: I find the resurrection story utterly baffling. If I actually sit down and think about it properly, I'm rendered speechless. Because I know, just as everyone else does, that dead people stay dead. But Jesus didn't. Jesus rose from the dead.

Read that again: Jesus rose from the dead.

He was dead – gone. Cold. Executed. Mortally wounded. He was wrapped in clothes and buried in a tomb. Dead. And then he was alive again. Warm. Breathing. Heart beating. Still bearing the scars of his execution, but somehow also alive. This is literally incredible. It makes no sense and, yet, somehow, it makes sense of everything.

Over the next fortnight, we're going to journey with Jesus' friends and disciples as they discover that actually, when it comes to Jesus Christ, dead people don't stay dead.

It's going to be a rollercoaster of a journey. We're going to meet doubters and deniers, believers and wonderers. We'll find empty tombs, broken hearts, tears shed, questions asked, questions answered, hearts mended, prayers prayed and doubts put to rest. We will see mourning turned to dancing, fear turned to joy and lives turned upside down and inside out, never to be the same again.

If you're anything like me, you're going to default to read this story as you've read it a thousand times before – slightly suspending reality, maybe reading it as you would a novel or a children's bedtime story. But can I encourage you, this year, to really take some time with it. Let it boggle your mind and mend your heart. Let it speak truth to your soul and put salve on your wounds. Because if Jesus really rose from the dead, nothing will ever be the same again. Wherever you are, whatever your circumstances and however you're feeling… this changes everything.

I don't know how you come to this Easter story. I don't know if you bring questions and doubts, fear or anger, pain or joy. But what I do know is that this story changes them all. This story brings hope to the hopeless, the angry, the hurting and the broken. It brings joy and peace to those who thought that they were lost forever.

Welcome to the most exciting, baffling, incredible, wonderful story ever told. Christ is risen; hope has arrived.

'Not here!'

'Why do you look for the living among the dead? He is not here; he has risen!' (NIV)

'Alleluia, the Lord is risen!'

The first Easter morning, however, was made up of less joy and more confusion. In fact, it began with great sadness. The women go to the tomb and 'took the spices they had prepared' – can you imagine how many tears fell into those spices as they chopped, pressed and mixed? Can you imagine the emotional weight these women were carrying, 'very early in the morning', as they went to anoint the body of their beloved rabbi?

But the body was not there – it had disappeared. And before they get any explanation, before the men with clothes that gleamed like lightning stood beside them, the women 'wonder about this'. I wonder *how* they wondered. Did they scream? Cry? Gasp? Did they fall to the ground? Were they talking to one another? Were they silent? What emotions did they feel? Fear? Sadness? A thrill of hope?

How do you feel as you walk this journey with these women? How do you feel when faced with the empty tomb?

The angels remind the women – Mary Magdalene, Joanna and Mary the mother of James – of what Jesus had said would happen, that he would be raised. And then they remember – and they go and tell others.

Unsurprisingly, they are not believed – not only because they are women, and thus not counted as credible witnesses at the time, but also because people knew then, just as we know now, that *dead people stay dead*.

But not with Jesus – with his resurrection, a new day has dawned. It feels unbelievable, too good to be true… and yet, as we journey through the resurrection appearances over the coming days, we will discover not only the empty tomb but also the risen Christ himself.

'He is risen indeed, Alleluia!'

Thank you, Father, for the empty tomb – teach me to wonder at its presence and to rejoice in its reality.

NELL GODDARD

'Mary'

He asked her, 'Woman, why are you crying? Who is it you are looking for?'… Jesus said to her, 'Mary.' (NIV)

Did you ever try that exercise where you say a sentence over and over again, with the emphasis on a different word each time? The classic one is 'I never said she stole my money' – its meaning changes with each emphasis.

Sometimes I do that with phrases in the Bible. Our English translation doesn't tell us which words are emphasised, and so it is left to our imagination. The angels' – and Jesus' – question to Mary: 'Woman, why are you crying?' is one such phrase. How was it emphasised? Was the main point the 'why', the 'you' or the 'crying'? Each one gives the sentence a different weight. Was it emphasised differently by the angels and by Jesus? Did one ask 'why' and the other focus on the 'crying'? I guess we'll never know, but it is a joy to mine the depths of those five short words, their meaning and their weight.

But the word I am most fascinated with in this passage is the name: 'Mary'. I want to know the tone in which Jesus said it. Was it a greeting? A consolation? A gentle rebuke? A shout? A sigh? Once again, we do not know. But what we do know is that Mary knew that voice as it said her name. She knew the timbre, the tone, the pitch. She knew the way he said her name. She recognised him by how he spoke her name, and she turned towards him.

How do you think the risen Jesus says your name? A greeting? A consolation? A gentle rebuke? A shout? A sigh? Maybe it is all of these. Maybe it is completely different. But when the Lord says your name, you cannot help but turn towards him.

Jesus, teach me to recognise your voice and to be so struck by the miracle of your resurrection that I turn towards you in wonder and awe.

NELL GODDARD

'They stole him away'

When the chief priests had met with the elders and devised a plan, they gave the soldiers a large sum of money, telling them, 'You are to say, "His disciples came during the night and stole him away while we were asleep."' (NIV)

It is a truth universally acknowledged that dead people stay dead. They don't break out of their grave clothes. They don't walk out of their tombs. And they certainly don't walk out of tombs blocked by large stones and guarded by Roman soldiers.

It's easy to understand that the Roman soldiers would have been panicked by this turn of events – this was unprecedented. So they do what any sensible worker would do in this situation, and head to their de facto line managers, the chief priests, to seek advice and help with the issue at hand.

But the chief priests are unhelpful – they meet with other management and decide to pay the soldiers to lie. No one will believe a story about an angel moving the stone away! No one will believe that a dead man came back to life! Tell them you were asleep, and the disciples stole the body. Don't worry about the fact that the story doesn't add up, and if you were asleep you wouldn't know whether the body was stolen. Don't worry about the fact that if the Roman authorities hear you were sleeping on duty, you'll be put to death… Here, have some money, keep shtum.

I've always judged the Roman soldiers in this story – how *dare* they spread such lies? How could they be so easily bought? But the truth is, we all have our price. I know I have mine.

So what's your price to stay quiet about the resurrection? Is it popularity? Intellectual kudos? Respectability? We may not be bought with a pile of gold coins, but we all have our reasons for not shouting the truth of the resurrection from the rooftops.

We all have our price for keeping quiet. What's yours?

Father, I'm so sorry for the times I have been 'paid off' to keep quiet about the truth of what you've done. Please give me the courage to speak about the resurrection and freely praise you for it.

NELL GODDARD

'Peace be with you!'

When the disciples were together, with the door locked for fear of the Jewish leaders, Jesus came and stood among them and said, 'Peace be with you!' After he said this, he showed them his hands and side. The disciples were overjoyed when they saw the Lord. (NIV)

As children, my brother and I used to try to come up with the funniest 'dying words' we could. From the sassy 'I told you I was ill' to the mysterious 'It's hidden under the fridge', much hilarity ensued as we considered possible parting words.

An upgrade of that game could be first words after resurrection: 'This is a surprise, perhaps?' Jesus' first words to his disciples as he appears to them in John's gospel, however, carry great and powerful weight: 'Peace be with you,' he says.

This is said to the disciples who had fled at Jesus' arrest; to one who had denied him; to two who had, earlier that day, seen the empty tomb and then headed back to safety; to those who had been told by Mary, 'I have seen the Lord!', but had nonetheless remained locked in a room, quaking in fear, unable to believe.

'Peace be with you,' Jesus says, as he appears with them. In the midst of denial and fear and confusion, Jesus appears and offers peace. And more than that, he shows them proof of who he is – nail-scarred hands, spear-pierced side.

And from the offer of peace comes joy. Maybe, just maybe, this is real. Maybe, just maybe, this is the beginning of something new. Maybe, just maybe, they have no need to fear. Maybe, just maybe, this peace is real. The rumours of resurrection are true. They, too, have seen the Lord.

'Peace be with you,' Jesus says. And his message of peace echoes down the ages and into today as he continues to appear in the midst of denial and fear and confusion.

Peace be with you.

Father, thank you that you offer us your peace – today and every day. May your offer of peace lead us, like the disciples, to deep joy and a firm belief in your presence and your power.

NELL GODDARD

'Stop doubting and believe'

'Unless I see the nail marks in his hand and put my finger where the nails were, and put my hand into his side, I will not believe'... Jesus told him, 'Because you have seen me, you have believed; blessed are those who have not seen and yet have believed.' (NIV)

I like to think of Thomas as offering the first-century equivalent of 'pics or it didn't happen', which is an internet saying used to counter unverifiable claims made online. Having heard the disciples speak of Jesus' bodily resurrection, Thomas – quite legitimately, I think – wants physical proof. He wants a personal encounter with the risen Lord Jesus.

A whole week passes between Thomas laying down the nature of his doubts and how they can be assuaged,and Jesus actually appearing to him again.

I wonder what the disciples – and particularly Thomas – were doing during that week. Were they praying together? Worshipping? Still hiding away in locked rooms? Were they trying to persuade Thomas of the reality of Jesus' resurrection? Or did they give up trying to reason with him after a couple of days? Did Thomas reach a point in that week where he thought he would never have his doubts put to rest?

What I love about this story is that Thomas doesn't doubt quietly. He doesn't exclude himself and slink away from the group of believers, but he stays in their midst, and he is honest about his doubts. And more than that – Jesus meets him in them. A week into his doubting, Jesus appears to him and answers his questions, fulfils his requests.

Jesus isn't afraid of our doubts, and we shouldn't be either. Thomas brings his doubt into the community and sits with it until his questions are answered. And Jesus does not admonish him for doubting – he merely praises those who 'have not seen and yet have believed'.

Doubt is a part of faith and not something to be ashamed of. Do not be afraid to bring your doubts to the risen Jesus, in the knowledge that he can – and will – put them to rest.

Lord, I believe. Help my unbelief.

NELL GODDARD

'How foolish you are!'

And beginning with Moses and all the Prophets, he explained to them what was said in all the Scriptures concerning himself. (NIV)

I find that walking with friends is one of the best ways to have a really good conversation, to put the world to rights, to thrash out issues and discuss big ideas. I imagine that's what Cleopas and his unnamed friend (possibly his wife) were doing as they took the seven-mile, two-hour walk from Jerusalem to Emmaus. They had so much to debrief from the last few days – Jesus' arrest and crucifixion, the hopes of Israel seemingly dashed, the rumours of angels and a missing body…

Deep in conversation, they are joined by a stranger who seems to know nothing of these happenings… and yet unpacks in full the meaning of what they have told him, as he 'explained to them what was said in all the Scriptures concerning himself'.

I wonder what Cleopas and his companion thought of this stranger, whom they were 'kept from recognising'. I wonder if they were baffled by him. Maybe they were annoyed at his rebuke, 'How foolish you are!' – I know I would have been. Perhaps they were perturbed by his explanation. Perhaps they were enraptured by his knowledge of the scriptures. I wonder how long it took before they fully grasped the breadth and depth of what they were hearing: God himself explaining salvation history as he walks along a dusty road.

What is your response to the claims of the risen Jesus – whether you recognise him or not? Are you baffled? Annoyed at his rebuke? Perturbed by his explanations? Enraptured by his knowledge? We may never fully grasp the breadth and depth of who he is and what that means, but may we continue walking along the dusty road with him by our side.

Father, give me eyes to see Jesus as he walks beside me. Give me a longing to learn of his presence throughout scripture. Give me joy as I realise his presence close.

NELL GODDARD

'It is true!'

When he was at the table with them, he took bread, gave thanks, broke it and began to give it to them. Then their eyes were opened and they recognised him, and he disappeared from their sight. (NIV)

I love Jesus and I love the gospels, but there are a number of situations that I read about where I can't help but think to myself, 'This must have been a really annoying thing for Jesus to do.' And this particular situation is one such scenario.

Far more frustrating than answering a question with a question (have you noticed how much he does this?), Jesus literally *disappears* as soon as Cleopas and his companion's eyes are opened to the reality of who he is. They must have had so many questions for him! So much to talk about, so much they wanted to get straight in their heads.

But I think it's worth noting that their recognition of Jesus was not a human recognition but a divinely given one – God opened their eyes. And when God opens your eyes, no one can shut them. I would imagine they knew with a deep certainty that this *was* the risen Christ and, despite their many logistical questions, that was all that mattered. Their hearts had been 'burning within' them as Jesus spoke, but their eyes had to be opened by God himself before they fully understood.

So convinced are they that they get up and head right back to Jerusalem – another seven-mile, two-hour walk… even though it was night-time. How excited they must have been! Jesus had been revealed to them in both word and sacrament – not only through his expounding of the scriptures but also through his breaking of bread.

The same is true today. We come to see the risen Jesus for who he is through God's opening our eyes, and we can rediscover him again and again in word and sacrament – in the Bible and in Communion. And we can pray that others would have this same experience.

Consider praying for a friend who has not yet recognised the risen Lord Jesus for who he is. Pray that God would open their eyes, and that they would have a lifetime of meeting Jesus in word and sacrament.

NELL GODDARD

'Why are you troubled?'

Jesus himself stood among them and said to them, 'Peace be with you.' They were startled and frightened, thinking they saw a ghost. He said to them, 'Why are you troubled, and why do doubts rise in your minds? Look at my hands and my feet. It is I myself!' (NIV)

Picture the scene: you are in the midst of hearing from two friends of an apparent resurrection appearance of your dead rabbi. The room is full of questions – 'Are you sure it was him?'; 'What makes you so certain?'; 'Tell us again *exactly* what he said?' – when suddenly the very person you are talking about appears in your midst.

'Peace be with you,' he says. It's reasonable that you would be 'startled and frightened' – more than a bit confused. Your heart would be racing. Who is this person? How did they get in? Why do they look like your dead friend? Could this possibly be true? Is he actually, really, truly resurrected?!

Jesus knows your concerns, your fears. And he – as he always does – meets you in them and calms the storm within. 'Look!' he says. Here's the proof: touch me and see; a ghost does not have flesh and bones, as you see I have. You may find all this hard to believe. And yet it is true – because remember what I said? Remember how I told you this would happen?

But… surely this is too good to be true? Dead people stay dead. They don't appear randomly in rooms and eat fish in front of you… do they? But Jesus does. You may still not grasp its truth 'because of joy and amazement', but it is true – Jesus is alive, and he is in the midst of your confusion, your fear, your doubt, your joy and your amazement.

Maybe, today, you still think the resurrection seems 'too good to be true'. But it is not. Praise God, for Christ is risen from the dead!

What is your initial response to the resurrected Christ? Amazement? Doubt? Confusion? Joy? Pray that God would show you the truth of his resurrection, and that you would know deep joy because of it.

NELL GODDARD

'This is what is written'

Then he opened their minds so they could understand the Scriptures. (NIV)

There is a woman in my parents' church who can barely read, who left school in her early teens and who only became a Christian a few years ago. And yet, when we sat down with her over lunch one day and started talking about the Bible with her, she made theological observations and declarations that were far beyond anything we could have imagined. Some of the things she said made even my dad – the one with a doctorate in theology – go, 'Ooh, I hadn't thought of that!'

My point is this: through his Holy Spirit, Jesus explains the scriptures to us, just as he did in person for the disciples when he appeared to them post-resurrection. He explained to them exactly what they would need to know in order to go and preach the truth of who he is and what he has done. He equipped them for the task set before them – these twelve young men with little or no formal education.

I can just imagine their amazement and delight as Jesus – God himself in human flesh, resurrected from the dead – sat with them and carefully explained exactly what it all meant. What a privilege! They had such knowledge to share now.

But with great power (and knowledge) comes great responsibility: 'You are witnesses of these things,' Jesus reminds them. And therefore, he is going to send them 'what my Father has promised', and they will later be given instructions to take the message out into the world.

God never leaves us ill-equipped. Whatever our circumstances or background, his word is living and active and, through his Holy Spirit, he can open our minds so that we, too, can understand the scriptures… and then we can go and share this good news.

Father, please open my mind so that I, too, can understand the scriptures. Thank you that you send your Holy Spirit to help me. Please teach me so that I can go and share the good news with others.

NELL GODDARD

'It is the Lord!'

Early in the morning, Jesus stood on the shore, but the disciples did not realise that it was Jesus. He called out to them, 'Friends, haven't you any fish?' 'No,' they answered. He said, 'Throw your net on the right side of the boat and you will find some.' (NIV)

What do you do when nothing has gone to plan and you don't know what to do next? Where do you go back to in order to feel safe and normal again? For Simon Peter, he went fishing. That was what he could do, that was what he was good at. Even during the resurrection appearances, I'm guessing Peter would have been feeling a bit odd, a little out of place. After all, he is the one who had denied knowing Jesus.

So, he goes fishing. He goes to do something that he knows he can do, somewhere he has to concentrate but he doesn't have to think.

And yet, it would seem, he can't even do that. Accompanied by two friends, they catch absolutely nothing. How disheartened they must have felt, how let down. Peter couldn't stick by his best friend, and now he couldn't even catch any fish. Couldn't he do anything right?

But then someone appears on the shore: 'Throw your net on the right side of the boat and you will find some.' But what does this stranger know about fishing? How dare he tell Peter how to do his job? Doesn't he realise that Peter has tried that already?

With nothing to lose, Peter tries it anyway. And suddenly there are more fish than he can count, more than the net should be able to take. And then, the realisation: 'It is the Lord!' says John.

Jesus has met Peter in failure, in stress and in disappointment. He stands on the shore and invites him to try something his way, to trust him. And Peter is amazed. Jesus does the same for us today. And there is no doubt that if we trust him, we, too, will be astounded at the result.

Father, thank you that you meet me where I am – no matter how I'm feeling. Please give me the courage to trust you.

NELL GODDARD

'Do you love me?'

When they had finished eating, Jesus said to Simon Peter, 'Simon son of John, do you love me more than these?' 'Yes, Lord,' he said, 'you know that I love you.' Jesus said, 'Feed my lambs.' (NIV)

It's a horrible feeling, isn't it? When you know that you have wronged a friend, but you're not entirely sure how to fix it. When you're spending time with them knowing you've hurt them, and knowing that they know, too. You so desperately want to clear the air, but you don't see how you can. And then there's that sense of relief when they take the plunge and finally bring it up. Relief coupled with fear… will they reject you? Will they admonish you? Is this the end of the friendship?

I imagine that's how Simon Peter felt as he ate breakfast with Jesus. Peter knew he had denied Jesus. Peter knew that Jesus knew. What next?

But Jesus does something remarkable. He turns to Peter and asks him a simple, heart-breaking question: 'Simon, son of John' – the equivalent of using someone's full name – 'do you love me more than these?'

What was there to say but what Peter did? 'Yes, Lord, you know that I love you.' And again Jesus asks. Again, Peter responds. And again.

There is plenty to be said about these three questions; plenty written on the language used. But what sticks with me about this encounter is that Jesus is kind. Peter has betrayed Jesus, he has denied him and he has hurt him. And yet Jesus is kind. He asks Peter three simple questions, and then he reminds him of his first instruction: 'Follow me!'

So simple, and yet so beautiful. Jesus offers a chance for Peter to be redeemed, to make amends, and then invites him to follow him once again.

And he does the same for us today. Jesus offers us a chance to be redeemed, to make amends, and then invites us to follow him once again.

Is there anything that you are feeling ashamed about in Jesus' presence? Bring it to him and ask him to redeem it in the way he redeemed Peter's shame and denial.

NELL GODDARD

'Go and make disciples'

'Therefore go and make disciples of all nations, baptising them in the name of the Father and of the Son and of the Holy Spirit, and teaching them to obey everything I have commanded you. And surely I am with you always, to the very end of the age.' (NIV)

I love how honest the Bible is. When the disciples see the risen Jesus for the first time in Matthew's gospel, we're told that 'they worshipped him; but some doubted'. How refreshing! And even more refreshing, Jesus gives this instruction to *all* those present, worshippers and doubters; doubt doesn't exclude us from his great commission.

Jesus instructs his disciples to do four things: go, make, baptise, teach. And then he makes a promise: 'I am with you always.'

'*Go*,' he says – Don't stay in your little disciple bubble, but break out and spread the news! '*Make disciples of all nations*' – To reach the nations, you have to leave Jerusalem. And you are to make disciples: train people to understand my message and to follow my way. '*Baptise them*' – for this is public witness that they are marked with the holy name – the Father, the Son and the Holy Spirit. '*Teach them* to obey everything I have commanded you' – This teaching is not abstract; it's moral, ethical and spiritual, and results in a lifestyle that looks different from the surrounding culture.

The verbs 'baptising' and 'teaching' are participles which are dependent on the main verb: 'make disciples'. They qualify it and make clear that making disciples is not complete until it leads those who have heard the news to a life of observing Jesus' commandments.

This is a big ask. But Jesus goes on – he does not leave the disciples (or us) on their own: 'And surely, I am with you always, to the very end of the age.'

Jesus never asks us to do anything without him. He is with us always. So it might be a big ask… but it's done in partnership with the king of the universe.

Father, thank you that as a result of other people obeying the great commission, I became a Christian. Give me the opportunities and the courage to do the same. Thank you that you have promised to be with me always.

NELL GODDARD

'The gift my Father promised'

On one occasion, while he was eating with them, he gave them this command: 'Do not leave Jerusalem, but wait for the gift my Father promised, which you have heard me speak about. For John baptised with water, but in a few days you will be baptised with the Holy Spirit.' (NIV)

'Your delivery is expected between 0900 and 1700 on Friday 16 April.'

I don't know about you, but I always find those texts quite frustrating. A whole eight-hour window? I always hope I'll be the first on the delivery driver's list... but of course I never am, and I end up waiting in the house the whole day.

What Jesus says to his disciples in this passage is a little bit like one of those texts: 'Don't leave Jerusalem, but wait for the gift my Father has promised.' There's something on its way to you, and you won't be able to do what I have told you to do without it. It is vital for your work... you just have to wait.

Jesus even gives a hint: 'For John baptised with water, but in a few days you will be baptised with the Holy Spirit.'

Now, perhaps I'm too much of a details person, but I always wonder what the disciples thought of that. Yes, Jesus often spoke in cryptic messages, so they were probably used to it, but there had been no real explanation of what the 'Holy Spirit' was. Was it something physical? Something emotional? Something metaphorical? What would it look like? How would they know when it had arrived? Did they have to wait in a particular location in Jerusalem for its arrival, or would it find them wherever they were?

The wonderful thing for us today, however, is that we do not have to wait for the Holy Spirit. As soon as we become a Christian, we have the Holy Spirit dwelling within us. There is no 'your delivery is expected' text, only a 'your delivery has arrived' message. We have received the Spirit – we have the presence of God living within us. What a joy!

What does it mean for you today to know that you already have the Holy Spirit dwelling within you? How might that change what you do today?

NELL GODDARD

'You will be my witnesses'

'You will be my witnesses in Jerusalem, and in all Judea and Samaria, and to the ends of the earth.' After he said this, he was taken up before their very eyes, and a cloud hid him from their sight. (NIV)

'Are you going to restore the kingdom to Israel?'

With that question, the disciples show that they still had great expectations for Jesus – they still expected him, as the Messiah, to overthrow the Roman authorities and to restore the kingdom to Israel. But once again they are wrong.

'You don't need to know,' Jesus says. Only the Father knows the time and the place of restoration. But what you do need to know, he explains, is that you will have power, and you will be my witnesses – in Jerusalem, in all Judea and Samaria, and to the ends of the earth.

God has authority; the disciples have power. And then comes Jesus' instruction: spread the news.

This is not about a geographical or political kingdom. The kingdom of God is international in its membership and gradual in its expansion – but it cannot be stopped. It has radical political and social implications, and it will change the world. And the disciples are to be witnesses to that. Don't gaze into the sky waiting for Jesus' return. Go, get on with spreading the news. That is your mandate.

They were probably suffering from slight emotional whiplash at this point: last supper, crucifixion, resurrection, post-resurrection appearances, the great commission and now this. They must have been feeling pretty exhausted. But tired as they were, they headed back into the city to 'join together constantly in prayer'.

Jesus hadn't conformed to their expectations; he hadn't – as far as they could see – restored the kingdom to Israel. All he had told them was to wait and to be a witness. And, as cryptic as those instructions were, the disciples still followed them. They went and prayed and sought his will, waiting for the Spirit to come. May we have the courage to do the same.

Father, teach me to acknowledge your authority, embrace the power you have given me, and go and make disciples.

NELL GODDARD

Made to worship

Amy Boucher Pye writes:

When I received the commission to write these notes on worship, I had the passing thought that a worship leader might be best placed to write them. But then I reminded myself that our life's main purpose is to worship God and that I shouldn't relegate worship to the time we spend praising him through singing with others. Of course we praise and worship during those times, and our lives in Christ would be so much poorer without them, but they aren't the exclusive way to worship God.

We are to give honour and glory to God in the mundane and in the wondrous. It's how God's created us – to worship him. After all, if we don't give our praise to him, we'll focus on something else: something idolatrous, as we see in our readings this week from the Old Testament. Again and again the Israelites turned from God, seeking fulfilment through other gods. When they got into difficulty, however, they returned to the true God. And each time, he welcomed them back. The Old Testament readings emphasise obedience over sacrifice, how to worship with abandon and the role of repentance.

In the second week we move to the New Testament and the freedom that Jesus gives to us in our worship. He becomes the focal point of our praise as God who became man. His promise to dwell with us by the Holy Spirit changes how we worship, for we are aided by God himself. He came not to negate the Old Testament but to fulfil it. Thus we are no longer required to offer sacrifices, for when he died on the cross he was the perfect sacrifice for our sins.

We also look at a couple of Paul's letters with his emphasis on offering our bodies as a living sacrifice and on enjoying the freedom God gives us within appointed limits. We end with an imagination-stretching look at worship through the book of Revelation.

I pray that our time together will strengthen us in our love for God and how we express that devotion. May you experience sustenance in the seasons of dryness and wonder in moments of rich communion.

No god but God

'You shall have no other gods before me. You shall not make for yourself an image in the form of anything in heaven above or on the earth beneath or in the waters below. You shall not bow down to them or worship them.' (NIV)

Have you ever noticed that in the Genesis account of creation and the garden of Eden, there's no mention of worshipping God? I believe that's because worshipping was so part of Adam and Eve's unfallen nature, with them in communion with God and he with them, that it didn't need to be stated. But then they sinned, and the world has never been the same. We're still created to worship, but we need God's help and reminders to keep him first in our lives.

Because God's people kept on sinning, he gave them ten rules to live by – the ten commandments. These rules would help them to flourish and grow, and the first rules centre on worship. But notice that in verse 1 of our reading the people received the commandments through God speaking them out to them. They would have heard them in an audible voice, straight from God. Later, however, the people asked Moses to be their intermediary. Perhaps their sin gave them such a sense of shame that they wanted some distance between themselves and God.

The first commandment is to honour and love God above all others, and the rules that follow focus on how the people should worship him only. Because God made his people for himself, he guards their allegiance. He knows they will stray but wants them to remain devoted to him.

What do you worship? What's your first thought when you wake? We can easily reach for our devices to see what's happened in the world (or in our world) and bypass God. Instead, as we set aside these days to explore the topic of worship, could you join me in seeking God first?

God of all creation, you have made me to worship you. Help me not to harbour love for idols, but to love you wholeheartedly.

AMY BOUCHER PYE

Loving and serving God

He is your praise; he is your God, who performed for you those great and awesome wonders you saw with your own eyes. (NIV)

We saw yesterday how God gave the Israelites the ten commandments. But they rebelled, and God later entrusted another set of tablets to Moses for the people. When Moses came down the mountain, shining with the radiance of being in God's presence, he once again gave the people the law. And he admonished them to turn to God fully, worshipping him only.

Note the active verbs in verses 12–13 that Moses uses when calling them back to God – they are to walk with God, love him, serve him, fear him and observe his commands. They are not to be passive in their allegiance to him. Nor are they to disobey him; after all, the God of gods loves and chooses them. They are to remove the hardened outer layers of their hearts as they bow before him.

How are we similar to the Israelites? We may not openly rebel against God, but perhaps we feel complacent in our journey with him. One way to rekindle our faith is by looking back on how God met us and loved us in the past. Keeping a gratitude journal can remind us about the specific incidents and experiences we noted down, our words bringing back a rush of memories. Looking back during testing times or those moments when we don't sense God's presence can turn our hearts back to worshipping him. Our emotions will follow our wills as we commit to serving and honouring him.

Take a few moments to ponder the times when you have felt close to God and those times when you have not. How did you grow in your faith through both seasons? Which season are you in now?

Loving Lord, when I feel like you are far from me, help me to remember how you poured out your love to me in times past. Strengthen my faith that I might worship you.

AMY BOUCHER PYE

Worship through obedience

'Does the Lord delight in burnt offerings and sacrifices as much as in obeying the Lord? To obey is better than sacrifice, and to heed is better than the fat of rams.' (NIV)

Saul held promise as the first king of the Israelites, but he let the power of his position feed his ego as he ignored some of God's commands. For instance, although he was supposed to defeat his enemies completely, he spared the king of the Amalekites; he also kept back the best of the livestock for his own purposes. He thought he knew better than God, ignoring the Lord's instructions. Because of this sin, God regretted making him king.

Saul may have thought he got away with his sneaky actions, for he reported to Samuel that he had taken care of matters. But Samuel, having heard from God, knew the true nature of Saul's heart. When Samuel announced that God rejected Saul as king, he defined what true worship is. For although Saul gave offerings and sacrifices to God, he didn't obey the Lord fully. True worship comes through surrender – God seeks obedience and faithfulness rather than the mindless following of rules.

The more we obey God, the more natural a habit it becomes. Our obedience muscle becomes stronger and more second nature with increased use. How might this work in your life? For a day or for a week, tell God that you want to obey him. Commit to following his rules and laws and ask for the inspiration of the Holy Spirit. And when you sense a nudge from the Spirit and discern that it's from him, don't put off obeying that nudge. Act on it, whether it's to close your mouth and stop your grumbling or to write the note to the friend who just came to your mind. And, yes, I'm telling myself to follow through on these things too!

'Our Lord never insists on obedience. He stresses very definitely what we ought to do, but he never forces us to do it. We have to obey him out of a oneness of spirit with him' (Oswald Chambers).

AMY BOUCHER PYE

With all our might

'Give praise to the Lord, proclaim his name; make known among the nations what he has done. Sing to him, sing praise to him; tell of all his wonderful acts. Glory in his holy name; let the hearts of those who seek the Lord rejoice.' (NIV)

King David knew how to lose himself in worship. As he danced before the ark of the Lord – the container holding the tablets of the law that symbolised God's presence with his people – he danced 'before the Lord with all his might' (2 Samuel 6:14). Ridicule didn't stop him from expressing his praise and worship to God.

He lived out what he commanded his people. Earlier in his story as king, soon after he was appointed, he made a special place for the ark of God. Calling upon the people to praise God, he shared a long psalm with them (which also appears in Psalms 96, 105 and 106).

As you read this song, note the call to action, as we saw on Monday. David urges them to praise God's name, to sing to him, to look to him for strength, to remember his miracles and to declare his glory to the nations. He exhorts them to focus on the wonders of God.

As I mentioned in the introduction, I wonder how often we define worship as solely the singing we do in a group setting. That's worship, but it's not the only means of praising God. As we see in this song of David, when we look back to God's 'marvellous deeds among all peoples' (v. 24), we worship him. And that recollection might be something we do in our own home or while on a walk in God's creation.

Why not take some time to express your love for God, whether through writing him a letter, penning a poem, going for a walk or praying with a friend? Or how about putting on some praise music and dancing with all your might? Are we prepared, like David, to be undignified before God (2 Samuel 6)?

Lord, I worship you! You are good and kind and loving. You look on me with joy. May I ever praise you as I remember the ways you've loved me.

AMY BOUCHER PYE

Worship through repentance

'Our kings, our leaders, our priests and our ancestors did not follow your law; they did not pay attention to your commands or the statutes you warned them to keep.' (NIV)

An important part of worship is repentance, both individual and communal. We need to bend our knees before God not only for the things we each do that fail him, but also to repent collectively, as we see in the book of Nehemiah.

God's people had been in exile and returned to Jerusalem, residing again in God's city. Nehemiah and Ezra led the rebuilding and restoration, including of the city walls. When the walls were intact, Ezra read the law of Moses to the people, and they rejoiced and worshipped God, lifting their hands and responding, 'Amen! Amen!' (Nehemiah 8:6). But hearing the law convicted them of their sins – their own and those of their ancestors. They confessed these sins to God, asking for a clean slate: they could only worship God fully once they rid themselves of what made them unclean.

One of my favourite prayer exercises is imaginatively praying at the foot of the cross of Christ. There we can name specific sins we've committed or those that have been done to us. Writing them out, we can leave them at the cross, asking God through his Son and Spirit to take them from us. And then we wait, asking God for his gifts of healing, love and affirmation. This exercise frees us from the weight of unconfessed sin, that which can drag us down and keep us from loving and serving God wholeheartedly. It's an exercise we can repeat during different seasons as we seek to remain pure before God.

Perhaps you could pray at the cross of Christ today, in your imagination or in front of a real cross. Or maybe you could spend some time praying for your church or local community, as modelled by Ezra and Nehemiah.

Lord Jesus Christ, you died that we might live. Your death brings us freedom and release from our sins. Help us to enjoy the freedom of forgiveness today.
AMY BOUCHER PYE

Ascribe to God glory

The Lord sits enthroned over the flood; the Lord is enthroned as King forever. The Lord gives strength to his people; the Lord blesses his people with peace. (NIV)

The psalms pulse with praise to God. The songbook through which we can voice our worship to God, it gives us words to express our wonder, amazement, gratitude and – yes – lament to the Lord. I chose Psalm 29 as the one to focus on because David wrote it solely for the praise of God.

David looks to nature as he stretches his imagination about how to communicate the glory and majesty of the Lord. He uses a thunderstorm to illustrate God's power. Scientists now understand that these storms can release 1.3 billion volts – a mind-boggling number. That amount of energy could supply all of the power of a city such as New York for 26 minutes (not that the energy could be harnessed, however). This majestic voice of God thunders over the waters, shakes the deserts and strips bare the forests. Even the world-changing flood of Noah isn't greater than God, for he 'sits enthroned' over it (v. 10).

And how should the people respond to this powerful and mighty God? We cry, 'Glory!' (v. 9). We give him our praise and worship. This is for all of us – even those who act as though they are more powerful than God (v. 1).

We might think that our civilisation is more advanced than that of David's, but we too can cower in fear over the streaks of lightning and the crash of thunder during a storm. The might of nature's elements can point us to the wonder that this God is all-powerful, yet holds us close to his heart as a shepherd cradles a lamb. May we worship him with joy and awe.

Creator God, help me to realise how little I am compared with who you are. As I lift my eyes to the heavens, I marvel at your great works of love and mercy.
AMY BOUCHER PYE

Sharing our songs of praise

'Give praise to the Lord, proclaim his name; make known among the nations what he has done, and proclaim that his name is exalted. Sing to the Lord, for he has done glorious things; let this be known to all the world.' (NIV)

This short chapter in the book of Isaiah – just six verses – contains two songs of praise which summarise the main themes of the rest of Isaiah's prophecy. The first song, verses 1–3, which covers the main theme of Isaiah 40—55, shares how God's grace helps his people to trust in him. The second song, verses 4–6, which covers the theme of chapters 56—66, exhorts God's people to make his wondrous deeds known among the nations. So much is packed into so few words!

Let's look at the first song: note how Isaiah speaks for God's people by giving them these songs to sing. They had sinned, which angered God, but he didn't turn his anger on to them; instead he brought them comfort.

How true for us, too, living after Christ died for us on the cross! God becomes our salvation because he sent his own Son to fulfil the requirements of the law. The Lord himself becomes our defence (v. 2). And we who are thirsty in a dry land come to the well of salvation and drink.

In the second song, Isaiah exhorts the people to share what God has done with those around them. Their wonder at how he saved them is not something for them to keep to themselves, but for them to 'shout aloud' (v. 6). And we too shouldn't fear sharing about how God works in our lives. We might think our friends who don't share our faith are therefore not interested. But we might be surprised. When I've dared to share from my experiences with friends in my local community, I've had some deep conversations with them.

Which of the two songs shall you sing today?

'You, God, are my God, earnestly I seek you; I thirst for you, my whole being longs for you, in a dry and parched land where there is no water' (Psalm 63:1).
AMY BOUCHER PYE

Loving our God; loving our neighbours

'Love the Lord your God with all your heart and with all your soul and with all your mind and with all your strength.' (NIV)

The Shema is one of the most important prayers for Jewish people; they recite it daily in their morning and evening prayers. It comes from Deuteronomy 6:4–5, Moses' command for God's people: 'Hear O Israel: the Lord our God, the Lord is one. Love the Lord your God with all your heart and with all your soul and with all your strength.' ('Shema' is close to the Hebrew word for 'hear'.) It is customary when praying this prayer for Jewish people to shield their eyes with their hand so that they can focus their minds and hearts on the prayer.

When Jesus was questioned by the Jewish leaders and teachers of the law, he confirmed the importance of this command to put God first and to worship him fully with heart, soul, mind and strength. During the debate, a wise teacher overheard the discussion about the resurrection and asked his own question – which is the most important commandment? Jesus answered with this text from Deuteronomy. He also added the command to love our neighbours as ourselves. The wise teacher didn't try to trip up Jesus or twist his words into a knot, and Jesus could see the worshipful state of his heart.

We can worship God through putting him first and committing our hearts and minds to him. But what about worshipping him through loving our neighbour? That becomes far more concrete and difficult, doesn't it? We could worship God through serving the exasperating acquaintance, slowing down to let someone pass us on the road or in the supermarket, making that cup of tea or cleaning up the mess that we didn't create. Why not make this kind of worship your mission today?

Lord, expand my definition of worship. I want to serve you throughout the day, in the glorious tasks and in the mundane. Help me to fix my eyes upon you.

AMY BOUCHER PYE

True worship

The woman said, 'I know that Messiah' (called Christ) 'is coming. When he comes, he will explain everything to us.' Then Jesus declared, 'I, the one speaking to you – I am he.' (NIV)

Many of us are familiar with the narrative of the Samaritan woman meeting Jesus at the well in the heat of the day – it's such a compelling story of grace and love. Jesus reaches out to a member of what was a hated race (the Samaritans) and initiates a conversation with a woman (when Jewish rabbis might not even speak to their wives or daughters in public), inviting her to enjoy life in the kingdom of God. But have you taken a closer look at their conversation about worship?

She notes that he is a prophet and that Samaritan and Jewish people differ on where they should worship God; some commentators wonder if she's trying to divert Jesus' attention from her sin – that she has had five husbands and that the man she's with is not her husband. Let's assume that with her question she's genuinely seeking after God and his ways. Jesus looks to her heart as he tells her that true worship will happen not at a place (either a mountain or a city) but will be done 'in the Spirit and in truth' (v. 24). Then Jesus makes a startling revelation to this outcast woman – he is the Messiah, the Christ. That is, he is the one they will worship. The Holy Spirit will enable people to worship the true God as embodied in Christ.

How amazing that Jesus would make this revelation to one sinful woman who came from a despised people! He shatters the cultural barriers back then and today. We all, whatever our background or whatever we've done, are welcome to worship him. May we do so with joy and abandon as we say, 'Come, hear about the one who knows everything about me!'

Lord Jesus, slake my thirst. Give me your true and living water, that I might find my fulfilment in you.

AMY BOUCHER PYE

Tempted not to worship

And he said to him, 'I will give you all their authority and splendour; it has been given to me, and I can give it to anyone I want to. If you worship me, it will all be yours.' Jesus answered, 'It is written: "Worship the Lord your God and serve him only."' (NIV)

We live in a world that is not as God intended it, and we, because of our wrongdoing, are not as God created us to be. After Satan successfully tempted Adam and Eve to sin, we also succumb to the evil one. But we have the help of the Son and the Spirit dwelling within us. We can therefore resist the devil, and he will flee from us.

Jesus models true godly behaviour. When Satan tempts him after his 40-day fast, he names Satan's fallacies and refuses to give into his lies. He knows that if he worships Satan even for a moment, he'll no longer be the perfect sacrifice and will not provide redemption. In refuting the evil one and his falsehoods, he points to God's word, speaking its truth.

Of course, none of us will be tempted by the devil in the way Jesus was; after all, we aren't God's own Son. But we all face the temptation to water down our worship of God. Perhaps we succumb to the evil one in subtle ways: we utter a little lie; we decide we can't be bothered with reading the Bible or praying; we feed our selfish desires without caring for others.

We can turn from these temptations through asking God for his help. God may answer our prayers through the encouragement of a new friend or through an existing relationship. He will meet us as we pray and read his word, even if we're so overwhelmed that all we can do is cry out to him or let the words of a psalm wash over us. As we cling to him, we will find relief and peace. The battle, though it will reappear, passes from us.

Lord Jesus Christ, you spoke truth to the devil and he fled from you. Help me to resist the evil one and to worship the Father through you.

AMY BOUCHER PYE

A living sacrifice

Therefore, I urge you, brothers and sisters, in view of God's mercy, to offer your bodies as a living sacrifice, holy and pleasing to God – this is your true and proper worship. (NIV)

Some sacrifices in the Old Testament atoned for sin. God's people would bring as perfect a specimen as they could find of a dove, bull or other animal. As the slaughtered animal was burnt at the altar, a pleasing aroma to God would follow.

When Jesus, God's own Son, died on the cross, he became the perfect sacrifice for our sins. No longer do we offer animal sacrifices, for his death covers the cost of our sins once and for all. But the apostle Paul, who was a leading Jewish thinker before his conversion on the Damascus Road, doesn't want followers of Christ to lose the richness of the sacrificial practice. As he urges the Roman Christians, we too are to offer our bodies as a living sacrifice to God; this is our act of worship.

Note how strongly Paul directs them. They are to use the strength of their wills, enriched by the indwelling of the Holy Spirit, to control their bodies. As they submit to God in their minds and hearts, their bodies will follow. And through the Spirit their minds will be transformed.

When we think about giving our bodies as a living sacrifice to God, we might protest that these earthly vessels are far from perfect, with our wonky hips or less than ideal weight. But we need not worry, for Jesus has stood in our place – he is the unblemished one. Our living sacrifices, with all of their imperfections, are enough.

One practical way of offering your body as a living sacrifice is to consider and pray about your relationship with food, drink or exercise. If you have a healthy approach to them, give thanks. If you need to work through some issues, you could start by bringing your fears and practices to God.

Lord, give me the strength and fortitude to offer my body to you as a living sacrifice, holy and pleasing to you. I want to worship you with all of my being.
AMY BOUCHER PYE

Freedom within the boundaries

So whether you eat or drink or whatever you do, do it all for the glory of God. Do not cause anyone to stumble, whether Jews, Greeks or the church of God – even as I try to please everyone in every way. (NIV)

I have a friendly debate with a Christian mate over halal meat, for he avoids eating it. I like to point to this passage in 1 Corinthians, citing Paul's teaching that we can eat whatever is sold in the butcher's for 'the earth is the Lord's, and everything in it' (v. 26, with Paul quoting from Psalm 24:1). My friend counters with Paul's words a few verses later in verse 28, that the label 'halal' implies a statement that the food has been offered in sacrifice and that we therefore should not eat it.

Whether you agree more with me or with my friend, I hope you can see that this discussion in Paul's letter to the Corinthians holds relevance for our lives today. We have freedom within the limits of what is honouring to God and others. When our actions cause others to stumble in their faith, we should refrain from doing them. But when they do not, we can embrace the freedom that Christ gives to us.

Focus on verse 31, where it says that whatever we eat or drink or whatever we do, all should be for the glory of God. This calls to mind the opening question of the Westminster Catechism, created in the 17th century, as to what is the 'chief end' of humanity. The answer: 'To glorify God, and to enjoy him forever.' As we enjoy our relationship with God, we bring glory to him. His mercy and love will flow in and through us, helping us to discern the right way forward in the daily matters of life, including what and what not to eat.

'Do you not know that your bodies are temples of the Holy Spirit, who is in you, whom you have received from God? You are not your own; you were bought at a price' (1 Corinthians 6:19–20).

AMY BOUCHER PYE

Holy, holy, holy

'You are worthy, our Lord and God, to receive glory and honour and power, for you created all things, and by your will they were created and have their being.' (NIV)

I emailed a friend today, someone I've not seen much recently. We rued the passing of time and how our paths hadn't often crossed. In my response, I said how I looked forward to the kingdom of heaven and how we'd have lots of time to catch up while enjoying the presence of God together. I knew that my comments could be interpreted as trite, but trusted she understood my longing for the communion of saints in heaven.

Our last look at worship together rightly focuses on a passage from Revelation, which gives us a snapshot of what heaven is like. John sees 'a door standing open in heaven' (v. 1) as God welcomes us in.

The sight detailed there might feel confusing or disconcerting – those living creatures covered in eyes, for instance. But as we slow ourselves down and read carefully, a picture of wonder and glory can emerge in our imaginations. I get weepy when I picture it.

Note how God isn't actually portrayed, except for the luminous light that emanates from him – he has the appearance of precious jewels, with an emerald rainbow surrounding him (v. 3). Around him are elders, who could be angels, but probably are God's children, living in their heavenly bodies with no faults or diseases.

The creatures and the elders never stop worshipping God, praising him for how holy he is and how worthy of our praise. He will always deserve our worship, for he will always be holy and true.

This passage would be a good one to read through meditatively and prayerfully. As you read it, ask God to highlight a word or phrase. Hold that word before you as you reread the passage, asking God for his gifts of wisdom and discernment.

Holy God, you are worthy of our worship and adoration! You created us in your image, and your love will never end. I give you glory, honour and praise!
AMY BOUCHER PYE

Enabling all ages to grow in faith

Anna Chaplaincy
Living Faith
Messy Church
Parenting for Faith

The Bible Reading Fellowship (BRF) is a Christian charity that resources individuals and churches. Our vision is to enable people of all ages to grow in faith and understanding of the Bible and to see more people equipped to exercise their gifts in leadership and ministry.

To find out more about our ministries and programmes, visit
brf.org.uk

Day by Day with God is on Instagram!

Follow us for a daily quote from *Day by Day with God*,
to help you meet with God in the everyday.

  Follow us: @daybydaywithgod

Were you there? BRF celebrates its centenary in 2022 and we'd love you to share your BRF memories with us. We've already heard from supporters with wonderful stories. Beryl Fudge attended our 25th anniversary service in Westminster Central Hall in 1947, in the presence of the Queen Mother and Princess Margaret. Catharine Heron was prepared for confirmation in 1945 by our founder, Canon Leslie Mannering, and still has his duplicated notes in their original brown cardboard folder.

Do you have a BRF story to tell, whether of events, people, books or Bible reading notes? Please email **eley.mcainsh@brf.org.uk**, call **01865 319708** or write to **Eley McAinsh** at BRF, 15 The Chambers, Vineyard, Abingdon, OX14 3FE, United Kingdom.

Recommended reading

Using the metaphor of pilgrimage, Sally Welch walks alongside us as leader and guide, but also fellow traveller, to explore how we can understand this biblical principle and make it our own. This book is divided into sections of a journey, beginning with the preparations necessary before setting out, exploring the obstacles which might be put in our path and sharing ways in which the journey can be made easier and more productive.

Journey to Contentment
Pilgrimage principles for everyday life
Sally Welch
978 0 85746 592 4 £8.99
brfonline.org.uk

TRYSTAN OWAIN HUGHES

OPENING OUR LIVES

Devotional readings for Lent

BRF LENT BOOK

Lent is not about giving up or taking up, but a radical opening up: the opening up of our lives to God's transformative kingdom. That is the challenge Trystan Owain Hughes sets in *Opening Our Lives*. Through practical daily devotions he calls on us to open our eyes to God's presence, our ears to his call, our hearts to his love, our ways to his will, our actions to his compassion and our pain to his peace.

Opening Our Lives
Devotional readings for Lent
Trystan Owain-Hughes
978 0 85746 882 6 £8.99
brfonline.org.uk

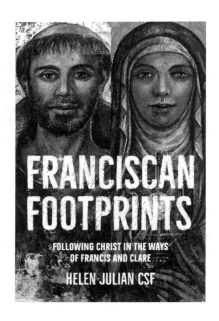

There are many ways of following Christ – each footprint is unique. One of these, the Franciscan spiritual journey, has been tried and tested over the centuries, and the experiences of St Francis and St Clare and all those who have been inspired by their lives still resonate with us. Helen Julian CSF explores the distinctive features of their spirituality and shows how these practices can be applied to, and become part of, our daily lives.

Franciscan Footprints
Following Christ in the ways of Francis and Clare
Helen Julian CSF
978 0 85746 811 6 £8.99
brfonline.org.uk

To order

Online: brfonline.org.uk
Telephone: +44 (0)1865 319700
Mon–Fri 9.15–17.30

Delivery times within the UK are
normally 15 working days. Prices are
correct at the time of going to press
but may change without prior notice.

Title	Price	Qty	Total
Journey to Contentment	£8.99		
Opening Our Lives	£8.99		
Franciscan Footprints	£8.99		
Day by Day with God (Jan–Apr 2021) – single copy	£4.70		
Day by Day with God (May–Aug 2021) – single copy	£4.75		

POSTAGE AND PACKING CHARGES			
Order value	UK	Europe	Rest of world
Under £7.00	£2.00		
£7.00–£29.99	£3.00	Available on request	Available on request
£30.00 and over	FREE		

Total value of books	
Postage and packing	
Total for this order	

Please complete in BLOCK CAPITALS

Title .... First name/initials .... Surname...

Address...

.... Postcode ....

Acc. No. .... Telephone ....

Email...

Method of payment

❑ Cheque (made payable to BRF) ❑ MasterCard / Visa credit / Visa debit

Card no. ☐☐☐☐ ☐☐☐☐ ☐☐☐☐ ☐☐☐☐

Expires end ☐☐ ☐☐ Security code* ☐☐☐ Last 3 digits on the reverse of the card

Signature* .... Date .... /............ /............

*ESSENTIAL IN ORDER TO PROCESS YOUR ORDER

Please return this form to:

BRF, 15 The Chambers, Vineyard, Abingdon OX14 3FE | **enquiries@brf.org.uk**
To read our terms and find out about cancelling your order, please visit **brfonline.org.uk/terms**.

The Bible Reading Fellowship (BRF) is a Registered Charity (233280)

Each issue of *Day by Day with God* is available from Christian bookshops everywhere. Copies may also be available through your church book agent or from the person who distributes Bible reading notes in your church.

Alternatively you may obtain *Day by Day with God* on subscription direct from the publishers. There are two kinds of subscription:

Individual subscriptions
covering 3 issues for 4 copies or less, payable in advance
(including postage & packing).

To order, please complete the details on page 144 and return with the appropriate payment to: BRF, 15 The Chambers, Vineyard, Abingdon OX14 3FE

You can also use the form on page 144 to order a gift subscription for a friend.

Group subscriptions
covering 3 issues for 5 copies or more, sent to one UK address (post free).

Please note that the annual billing period for group subscriptions runs from 1 May to 30 April.

To order, please complete the details on page 143 and return with the appropriate payment to: BRF, 15 The Chambers, Vineyard, Abingdon OX14 3FE

You will receive an invoice with the first issue of notes.

All our Bible reading notes can be ordered online by visiting
brfonline.org.uk/collections/subscriptions

Day by Day with God is also available as
an app for Android, iPhone and iPad
brfonline.org.uk/collections/apps

Follow us on Instagram: **@daybydaywithgod**

All subscription enquiries should be directed to:
BRF, 15 The Chambers, Vineyard, Abingdon OX14 3FE
+44 (0)1865 319700 | **enquiries@brf.org.uk**

DAY BY DAY WITH GOD GROUP SUBSCRIPTION FORM

> All our Bible reading notes can be ordered online by visiting
> **brfonline.org.uk/collections/subscriptions**

The group subscription rate for *Day by Day with God* will be £14.25 per person until April 2021.

☐ I would like to take out a group subscription for .... (quantity) copies.

☐ Please start my order with the May 2021 / September 2021 / January 2022* issue. (*delete as appropriate)

Please do not send any money with your order. Send your order to BRF and we will send you an invoice.

Name and address of the person organising the group subscription:

Title .... First name/initials .... Surname ....

Address..

.... Postcode ....

Telephone .... Email ....

Church..

Name and address of the person paying the invoice if the invoice needs to be sent directly to them:

Title .... First name/initials .... Surname ....

Address..

.... Postcode ....

Telephone .... Email ....

Please return this form to:
BRF, 15 The Chambers, Vineyard, Abingdon OX14 3FE | **enquiries@brf.org.uk**

To read our terms and find out about cancelling your order, please visit **brfonline.org.uk/terms**.

The Bible Reading Fellowship is a Registered Charity (233280)

DAY BY DAY WITH GOD INDIVIDUAL/GIFT SUBSCRIPTION FORM

To order online, please visit **brfonline.org.uk/collections/subscriptions**

☐ I would like to give a gift subscription (please provide both names and addresses)
☐ I would like to take out a subscription myself (complete your name and address details only once)

Title .... First name/initials .... Surname ....

Address ....

.... Postcode ....

Telephone .... Email ....

Gift subscription name ....

Gift subscription address ....

.... Postcode ....

Gift subscription (20 words max. or include your own gift card):

....

....

Please send *Day by Day with God* beginning with the May 2021 / September 2021 / January 2022 issue (*delete as appropriate*):

(please tick box)	UK	Europe	Rest of world
1-year subscription	☐ £18.00	☐ £25.95	☐ £29.85
2-year subscription	☐ £35.10	N/A	N/A

Total enclosed £ .... (cheques should be made payable to 'BRF')

Please charge my MasterCard / Visa credit / Visa debit with £ ....

Card no. ☐☐☐☐ ☐☐☐☐ ☐☐☐☐ ☐☐☐☐

Expires end ☐☐☐☐ Security code* ☐☐☐ Last 3 digits on the reverse of the card

Signature* .... Date ...... / ...... / ......
*ESSENTIAL IN ORDER TO PROCESS YOUR ORDER

Please return this form to:
BRF, 15 The Chambers, Vineyard, Abingdon OX14 3FE | enquiries@brf.org.uk

To read our terms and find out about cancelling your order,
please visit **brfonline.org.uk/terms**.   The Bible Reading Fellowship is a Registered Charity (233280)